INDISPENSABLE HANDY BOOKS.

GARDENING

AND

MONTHLY
CALENDAR OF OPERATIONS

GIVING

PLAIN AND PRACTICAL INSTRUCTIONS

IN THE CULTIVATION OF

Fruit, Flower, and Kitchen Gardens

AS WELL AS

HOW TO LAY THEM OUT TO THE BEST ADVANTAGE
FOR BEAUTY AND PROFIT.

LONDON:
WARD & LOCK, 158, FLEET STREET.
M DCCC LXI.

PREFACE.

It is scarcely requisite to say anything in favour of such a delightful recreation as Gardening. A love of flowers and gardens seems to be a part of our common nature, implanted in almost every breast—in almost every clime. There is something pleasing in the very sound of the word *garden*—for it reminds us of flowers and fruits; and there is something so refining and so humanising in its practice and associations.

It is not for those alone who possess gardens that this HANDY BOOK is prepared. There is a description of gardening practicable by all who have a dwelling, be it ever so humble — which delights the impoverished weaver of Spitalfields as well as the wealthy denizen of a West-end square—cheers the lone tenant of the sick chamber, or sheds a lustre on the gaiety of the crowded ball-room.

As many persons no doubt are deterred from adding to their enjoyments by keeping plants, not only on account of being ignorant of their proper management, but also alarmed by the *imaginary* difficulty of acquiring a sufficient knowledge of the subject, it affords us great pleasure to set forth in this Volume plain and practical Monthly Instructions in untechnical language, and to show not only *when* to plant, sow, prune, but also *how* to perform these interesting operations. This Volume will not be a mere Calendar of Operations, but an Epitome of Gardening. We do not write for the wealthy, who have large establishments and employ gardeners, though even they may derive information from its perusal; but for those who cultivate their own gardens. Though wealth is very unequally distributed, yet the true blessings of Providence are enjoyable by all. The poor man receives as much pleasure from his pinks or pansies as the noble duke from his vines or palms. More so, in fact; for the poor man has bestowed his own pains and industry on the cultivation of his plants; and we all know, that without trouble we cannot reap enjoyment.

HANDY BOOK

OF

GARDENING;

AND

CALENDAR OF OPERATIONS.

BEFORE we commence our Monthly operations, we think it judicious to submit the following practical

MAXIMS FOR GARDENERS.

Grow nothing carelessly; whatever is worth growing at all, is worth growing well.

Many kinds of garden-seeds lose their vegetative power if kept over the first year; be sure, therefore, to sow none but new seeds.

Melons, cucumbers, and other plants of the gourd tribe, form an exception to this rule; their seeds should not be sown until they are several years old, for they will then produce plants with scanty foliage, but abundant fruit.

The seeds of most weeds will retain their vegetative power for an unlimited number of years: take care, therefore, that all weeds are burnt, or at all events that they are not thrown on piles, from which they are liable to be brought back to the garden.

The first leaves which appear in the seed-bed (called the seed-leaves) are the sole nourishment of the young plant until it has acquired roots; therefore, if they be destroyed or seriously injured, the young plant must die.

B

Seeds will not vegetate unless within the influence of moisture, air, and heat; be careful, therefore, not to sow your seeds too deep, or they will never come up.

Little good is obtained by saving your own seed from common annuals and vegetables; your ground is worth more to you for other purposes than the cost of the quantity of seed which you will require; besides which, you will have a better crop from seed raised in a different soil.

The roots of very young plants are not strong enough to bear removal: the best time for transplanting seedlings is when they have made from four to six proper leaves; for by this time the roots will be able to perform their proper functions.

Plants when exposed to the action of light, transmit moisture copiously through their leaves; transplanted seedlings, therefore, and cuttings, should be shaded from the sun till their roots are strong enough to supply moisture as rapidly as it is thrown off.

Roots require that air should be admitted to them; the surface of a clayey soil should therefore be disturbed as often as it begins to cake.

Let unoccupied ground be left in as rough a state as possible during the winter, in order that a large surface may be exposed to the frost, and the soil become thoroughly loosened.

Frost takes effect more readily on roots that have been dug up than on those which are left in the ground; therefore, either give your store roots complete protection, or let them stay in the ground.

All plants absorb from the ground different juices; a constant variation of crops is therefore indispensable.

Leaves absorb and give out moisture, and inhale and exhale air; they are consequently the most important organs of a plant, and if they are destroyed or injured, the whole plant suffers.

The pores in the leaves of the plants, by which they

transmit moisture and air, are exceedingly minute, and liable to be choked by exposure to dust, and especially soot; delicate plants should therefore be placed out of the reach of smoke, and if their leaves become soiled they should be washed.

The branches and leaves of plants rarely touch one another while in a growing state; learn from this not to crowd plants too much in your beds; air and light are as necessary to them as earth and water.

The throwing off of its leaves by a newly-planted cutting is a sign that growth has commenced; on the contrary, when leaves wither on the stem, it is a sign that the plant has not strength to perform the natural function of throwing them off.

When shrubs produce an abundance of foliage but no flowers, either move them to a poorer soil, or cut through some of the principal roots.

Dry east winds are injurious, by absorbing moisture from the leaves of plants more rapidly than they are prepared to give it out; weather of this kind requires to be guarded against more than the severest frost.

If a grass-plot becomes overrun with moss, manure the surface, and the grass will gain strength so as to overcome the intruder.

In all cases of pruning, cut towards you, beginning a little below a bud, but on the opposite side, and ending just above the bud; by this means the wood will be kept alive by the bud, and no water will be able to settle and rot on it.

Leaves shaded from the light do not acquire depth of colour or strength of flavour; gardeners take advantage of this fact, tying up lettuces and earthing celery, that they may be white and mild.

Light is necessary to flowers, that they may acquire their proper hues; therefore, when kept in rooms, their place should be as near as possible to the window.

All plants have a season of rest; discover what season is peculiar to each, and choose that season for transplanting.

Plants are in their most active state of growth while in flower; avoid transplanting them at this period, for in all probability they will suffer from the check.

On the contrary, choose this period, in preference to any other, for taking cuttings, as they are then most active in forming roots.

Plants when in bloom have all their juices in the most perfect state; choose, therefore, the period of their beginning to flower for cutting all aromatic and medicinal herbs.

Profuse flowering exhausts the strength of plants; therefore remove flower-buds before they expand from all newly-rooted cuttings and sickly plants.

No plants can bear sudden contrasts of temperature: therefore bring nothing direct from a hot-house to the open air; warm weather should be chosen even for bringing out plants from a greenhouse.

Remove all dead flowers from perennials, unless you wish to save seed; the plants will thus be prevented from exhausting themselves.

To procure a succession of Roses, prune down to three eyes on all the branches of some trees, as soon as the buds begin to expand; defer the same operations with others, until the leaves are expanding; in the former case the three buds will bear early flowers; in the latter they will not begin to expand until the others are in full foliage, and will bloom proportionally later.

By checking the growth of plants, you throw strength into the flowers and fruit; this is the reason why gardeners nip off the terminal shoots of beans and other such vegetables; on this principle, too, is founded the valuable art of pruning.

Generally speaking, the smaller the quantity of fruit on a tree, the higher the flavour: therefore, thin all fruits in moderation, but avoid excess; a single gooseberry on a tree, or a single bunch of grapes on a vine, no matter how fine it may be, is a disgrace to good gardening.

Fruit should always be gathered in dry weather, and carefully placed in baskets, not dropped in: the slightest bruise will cause fruit to decay.

All bulbs and tubers should he placed in the ground before they begin to shoot; if suffered to form leaves and roots in the air, they waste strength.

Never remove the leaves from bulbs after flowering until they are quite dead; as long as the leaves retain life, they are employed in preparing nourishment and transmitting it to the roots.

Vegetables that are valued for their juiciness and mild flavour should be grown quickly; the reverse should be the case when a strong flavour is required.

Though rapid growth is desirable in succulent vegetables, this is not the case with most flowering shrubs, which form bushy and therefore handsomer plants when grown slowly.

Few plants thrive in stagnant water; potted plants should, therefore, always have a thorough drainage of broken pots or brick, and should not be allowed to stand in damp saucers; they require but little water during the winter; but when they begin to grow they should be liberally supplied.

Plants in pots are more liable to be injured by frost than plants in the ground which are exposed to the same temperature, because the fibres of their roots cling to the sides of the pots and are soon affected; if they are kept out of doors during the winter, bury the pots in the ground.

All garden hedges should be kept clear of weeds, or when the latter run to seed, they will supply your garden with a stock against next season.

Finally, whether you sow seeds, water the young plants, or reap the produce, remember that you are dependent for all on God's blessing.

GARDENING FOR JANUARY.

FLOWER GARDEN.

TULIPS, Hyacinths, and all hardy bulbs, should have been planted in November. If any, through neglect, are still out of the ground, plant them immediately. Protect half-hardy plants by laying ashes over their roots, and cover with litter.

Window Gardening.

All tender plants in pots should be kept dry, not too warm, just free from frost, in fact, in nearly a torpid state. Oleanders, Scarlet Geraniums, Verbenas, Cacti, with all of the succulent tribe of plants, should not have one drop of water at this season. If you should, improperly, have any plant in a very dry place, a warm kitchen for instance, and they appear shrivelled, you may administer a very small quantity of water to them. Hydrangeas, if very dry, should have a little water. Camellias should be in a room where there is a fire; water them with great circumspection, never permitting them to become too wet or too dry. Keep them in a window as near the light as possible, but do not in sunny days allow the sun to shine directly upon them.

KITCHEN GARDEN.

Early Peas may now be sown in a dry soil and sheltered spot, but at the risk of losing them. Little is gained in small gardens by too premature work. Beans—the early kinds—should now be sown; the best way, for a small garden, is to sow in a bed and transplant into rows. Having selected a piece of ground for the bed, draw off the surface

earth with a spade or hoe to the depth of two inches : lay the
seeds all over the bed a square inch apart, cover evenly
with the mould drawn off, and tread it down firmly.
When the plants are about two inches high, ease them gently
out of the bed with all their roots, and as much soil as possible adhering to them; cut off the parent beam, and
shorten the tap-root (the tap-root is the long main root generally descending perpendicularly into the earth): plant them
four inches apart, in double rows, the rows nine inches apart,
and about three feet, not less, between the double rows ;
water when you plant, and close the earth well up about the
stems. As the plants grow up, earth up lightly, and water
when requisite. When the first blossoms are beginning to
fade, cut off an inch and a half at the top of the plant. For
the early crops the best sorts are the Mazagan and early
long pod ; for the full crop, the Windsor. One pint of seed
will sow about forty feet of row. The bean is a native of
the East, and is supposed to have been introduced to this
country by the Romans.

FRUIT.

In mild weather, you may prune Apples, Pears, Plums,
Cherries, Gooseberries, Currants, and Raspberries.

Pruning is the great bugbear of the tyro in gardening,
and is often very badly performed by the blue-aproned
jobbing *gardeners*, as they term themselves, who infest the
suburbs of London. Many fine trees, to my certain knowledge, do these men spoil annually. Now, there is no witch-
craft—no high art—required to enable any one to prune a
tree properly; all that is necessary, is to consider the *ra-
tionale* of the operation, and to observe the mode of bearing
of the tree or shrub that is to be pruned. I cannot better
describe the *theory* of pruning than in the words of London:—

He says—"Of two adjoining and equal-sized branches of
the same tree, if one be cut off, that remaining will profit by
the sap which would have nourished the other, and both the

leaves and fruits which it may produce will exceed their natural size. If part of a branch be cut off which would have carried a number of fruits, those which remain will set or fix better, and become larger." The object of pruning, then, we see, is to adjust the stem and branches of the tree to the nourishment it extracts from the soil by means of its roots; though, as all trees do not produce their fruit in the same manner, we must modify the general object of pruning according to the mode of bearing of the particular tree. For instance: we will begin with the Apple-tree, which produces its fruit on small terminal or lateral spurs, or short stout shoots, from one to two inches long, appearing first at the extremity, and extending gradually down the side of the branch, the branches and fruit-spurs remaining many years fruitful. Therefore, on the theory of pruning above-mentioned, we must cut out all superabundant and irregular young shoots, all decayed branches, shorten all irregular and too-far-extended branches; and keeping in view the mode of bearing of the tree, we must preserve all eligible natural fruit-spurs. Pears produce their fruit in the same manner as Apple-trees, consequently they require the same mode of pruning; but, as they are seldom encumbered with superfluous branches, they more rarely need it. Plum-trees have also nearly the same mode of bearing as the Apple; as their branches and spurs do not continue fruitful for so many years, you must leave more young shoots to come on, as successional bearers, than you do when pruning the Apple. Cherries, with the exception of the Morello, produce their fruit upon small spurs and studs, which proceed from the sides and ends of branches that are about two years old, new spurs continuing to shoot from the ends of the branches. Remove any cross-placed and crowded branches or shoots, and never shorten a branch when you have room to extend it. Gooseberries produce their fruit on shoots of a year old and upwards, also on spurs growing from the elder branches; cut out all cross and watery shoots of the previous summer's growth; shorten all rambling shoots; remove all decayed wood; retain a sufficiency of last year's shoots to form successional bearers.

Red Currants—Mode of bearing and pruning similar to gooseberries. Black Currants bear on the shoots of the preceding year, and spurs; prune as gooseberries, annually cutting out the old wood to make room for the new. Raspberries produce their fruit on the wood of the same year's growth; cut out the old dead stems; cut away the superabundant young shoots, retaining a few of the strongest; shorten these to three or four feet, according to their strength, and tie them together at the top.

GENERAL OBSERVATIONS.

Trench, or turn up into ridges, all vacant ground. Avoid digging when the ground is wet. Sweep up all dead leaves. Collect weeds, road-scrapings, and turves, for manure and compost. Though you cannot have your garden *gay* at this season of the year, yet you should have it *neat;* nothing is so unsightly as an ill-kept, untidy garden.

GARDENING FOR FEBRUARY.

FLOWER GARDEN.

ALL Perennials should now be transplanted to wherever it is intended they are to flower. Propagate perennials by dividing their roots. This method of propagation may be practised on nearly all hardy herbaceous plants. The plant may either be taken up, divided with a knife, and the portions replanted in their allotted places; or the earth may be partially removed, and part of the fibrous roots, and crown or body of the root cut off to form the new plant. The crown and eye are, in most roots, the only parts that can produce a stem; and roots are only capable of being pro-

pagated by division when they have more crowns or eyes
than one. In many plants the different crowns may be
separated by hand, breaking or pulling them asunder, with
a good portion of the fibres attached to each division; being
thus well provided with roots, they will grow without
difficulty. Other plants, such as Peonies and Dahlias,
cannot properly be separated by hand; and for these a
sharp knife should be used, cutting off the crown or eye
without tearing or bruising the parts. Each dvision should,
if possible, have a piece of the body of the root, and also
some of the fibres. This is not indispensable; for the
crown or eye alone, in a few instances, will grow without
possessing fibres at the time of planting; but the fibres
will, in scarcely any instance, succeed without having some
part of the body of the root attached to them. The chief
point, then, in the propagation of plants by dividing their
roots, is to make sure that each division has a few fibres,
and either a bud or eye, or the rudiment of one.

Ranunculus and Anemone Roots.

As Ranunculuses and Anemones require the same
treatment, the following directions are applicable to both.
These flowers show to the best advantage in beds. We
will describe the manner of planting, premising that detached plants should be managed the same way :—

The most suitable soil is a rich loam, with a slight
admixture of well-rotted dung. Your bed being well
dug, and raked fine, draw shallow drills, two inches
deep and six inches apart all over it. Place the roots in
the drills five inches apart—the Ranunculus roots with their
claws downwards, and the Anemone roots with that side
downwards on which you observe the decayed rudiments of
small thread-like fibres. When the roots are all placed,
fill up the drills level with the surface of the bed, the roots
being covered by not more than one inch and a half of
soil. When they appear above ground, press the earth

firmly round the root of each plant ; water freely in dry
weather ; and when the flowers expand, if a light shading
be afforded them, they will continue longer in bloom, and
preserve their colour better. After they have flowered,
the leaves will decay ; then take up the roots, carefully remove the soil from them, dry, and put them away for next
season : they should not be kept in a damp place. The
young offsets should be detached from the roots about a
month after they are taken from the ground—planted in
October, they will probably flower the ensuing year ; they
may then be treated in every respect as the old plants.
Protect all half-hardy plants, as in last month.

Prune Roses.

Prune one-half of your Roses now, the other half next
month, which will retard the blooming ; so when your first
pruned Roses are going out of flower, your second will be
coming in. Pruning is a most important operation in the
cultivation of Roses ; when neglected the flowers degenerate, and the stems become bare and unsightly. As the
different species of Roses vary considerably in their habits
and modes of bearing, the same treatment is not suitable
for all. China roses will not bear pruning ; their shoots
should never be shortened ; for, being of a soft pithy
nature, those which are pruned almost invariably die at the
extremities, making a very ugly appearance. You may cut
out all weak sprigs and branches, and after the main shoots
have flowered for two or three seasons, cut them out to
make room for the young ones that are yearly produced, the
young shoots always flowering the best. Cabbage or Provence, French, and Moss Roses, all require the same treatment. With these kinds you must not spare the knife.
Shorten the strong roots to about six inches, the weaker
ones to about three inches. Suckers—the new stems that
these Roses annually produce from under ground—to
within six inches ; when the suckers get on so as to flower

well, the old parts of the bush should be cut out altogether, the suckers succeeding each other in annual rotation. Scotch Roses should never be pruned, except to head down the rank and luxuriant suckers; they should be annually headed down until they are fit to take the place of the old wood, which should then be cut out. When pruning Roses, use a sharp knife, making a slanting upward cut, just above, but clear of a bud; if the rose is against a wall, always make the cut on the side of the stem that is next the wall. Standard Roses—those beautiful objects, which no one should be without who possesses a spot of ground—must be pruned closer still, cutting the young shoots back to within two or three buds of the old wood; as the chief beauty of Standards consists in their round, compact, bushy head, this should be kept in view when pruning. Roses should now be planted and moved as required—they delight in a rich loamy soil.

Window and Conservatory.

Still keep the plants dry, and give all the air you can. On fine days, towards the end of the month, you may turn the more hardy plants out in the sunshine, by way of an airing, for a few hours, watering them sparingly. Camellias as last month. Mignionette, Intermediate or Ten-Week Stocks, Sweet Peas, and all hardy annuals may now be sown in pots for flowering early in the season. The main thing, when sowing seeds in pots, is to secure proper drainage; for this purpose, place an oyster-shell, or a rounded piece of potsherd, over the hole in the bottom of the pot, then fill to about the fourth of the depth of the pot with potsherds, the larger pieces underneath, the smaller on the top. If you have not potsherds, pebbles will do, but not so well, and if for plants that are very susceptible of injury from damp, you must use coarse cinders. For Mignionette take a six-inch pot, that is, a pot six inches in diameter at the rim; having placed the drainage of potsherds,

fill the pot up with light rich soil to within half an inch of
the rim, leaving that space for the convenience of applying
water when necessary; slightly dampen the soil, and strew
about twenty seeds over it, covering them scarcely a quarter
of an inch (all young beginners at gardening sow seeds too
deep); as the plants come up and crowd each other, thin out
the weakest, leaving not more than eight or nine in each
pot—if you intend the plants to flower in the pot, four or five
will be sufficient. Ten-week Stocks may be raised the same
way, but in four-inch pots, leaving not more than four
plants in each pot; keep the pots in the window of a room
where there is a fire, and let them have all the light you
can. As the young plants advance in strength, place them
outside the window in the sunshine, or when mild gentle
rain is falling, taking them in at night, and watering them
when required. You may either let them flower in the pots,
or towards the latter part of April turn them out—keeping
the ball of earth unbroken—into the open garden. In
London a very general plan is to turn them out into window
boxes, a pot of each until the box is full; so when in flower,
the Stock alternating with the Mignionette has a very pretty
effect. Give water copiously when you turn the plant out.
Sweet Peas require much the same treatment, but must be
grown in larger pots, say from eight or nine inches in
diameter. Sow the peas in a circle, an inch from the side
of the pot; as they grow up, first give them small twigs to
cling to, and as they still progress larger sticks. They require plenty of water, and should be flowered in the pot.
Cinerarias, to flower in the autumn, should be sown early in
this month. Sow in four-inch pots, well drained with
coarse cinders, the soil a light sandy loam; treat as we
have directed for Mignionette, but remember that the Cineraria is more tender; as they come up, thin out to four
plants in each pot; in a short time they will be large enough
to require separate pots; transplant them then, each into a
four-inch pot, give them a richer soil, and as they advance,

transplant again into larger pots, if they seem to require it.
When they flower, save the seed from the best plants to sow
again next year. By this method of treating Cinerarias as
annuals, you have more room for other plants in their
winter quarters—a very great object to the window gardener. Before you sow seeds in pots, soak the pots in water
for a night, if you do not do so, the porous nature of the pot
will suck all the genial moisture from the seeds and soil.

KITCHEN GARDEN.

Cabbages, to come in as a young summer crop, and part to
stand the winter, should be sown from about the 15th of
this month to the 1st of April. Sow moderately thick in an
open situation, raking the seed in evenly, lengthways in the
bed. When the plants have two or three leaves an inch or
two broad, thin out one-half from the seed-bed, transplanting them into a bed of good earth, about four inches apart,
giving water. When of suitable growth for final transplanting in May, June, or July, they should be planted out
in a well-manured and fresh-dug plot. The rows for the
dwarf kinds may be a foot apart, and the plants nine inches
apart in the row. For the larger sorts, the rows should be
a foot and a-half apart, and the plants a foot apart in the
row. When transplanting, if you observe any little knobs
on the roots, cut them off with a sharp knife; also cut off
an inch or two from the end of the tap-root. Water freely
when you transplant, and press the earth close up to the
roots with the dibble. For a seed-bed ten feet long and
four feet wide, an ounce of seed will be sufficient.

Peas.

Early Peas may be sown in the last week of this month.
Having prepared the ground, draw drills three inches deep
and nine inches apart, to form a double row; the double
rows for the dwarf kinds should be three feet, and for the
taller-growing sorts four, five, six, and seven feet asunder,

according to their height of growth. Sow the seed pretty thick in the drills, and let them be as level as possible, so that your crop may be of an equal height: cover with the earth taken out of the drills, and tread it down firmly. As the plants advance, earth up, and keep free from weeds; when the tendrils appear, place rods along the rows. Half a pint of seed will sow ten yards of row.

Potatoes.

The only indisputable feature in the mysterious disease that affects this useful root is, that early sorts, early planted, almost always escape its visitation.

Radishes.

After planting potatoes rake the ground smooth, and sow radishes over them; the radishes will be fit for pulling before the potatoes are above the ground. For a bed three feet broad and nine feet long, an ounce of seed is sufficient.

FRUIT.

Fruit trees of all kinds may be planted. Prune Apricots, Nectarines, and Peaches, before the buds are much swollen. Finish all your pruning this month. Apricots generally bear on the young shoots of last year, and spurs on the two and three year old branches. Cut off irregular, superfluous, and cross-placed branches, and any old unfruitful wood. Peaches and Nectarines bear on the wood of a year old, the same shoot seldom bearing a second year. Hence you must retain a sufficient supply of young shoots to come on in succession; cut out decayed wood and unfruitful branches.

GENERAL OBSERVATIONS.

All the winter work of the garden left undone should now be got over as soon as possible, before the busy time of sowing commences. Walks, where wanted, should be made. The whole art of making a gravel walk consists in having a good foundation of broken bricks, lime rubbish, &c., previous to laying on the gravel. The walk should be made with a slight rise in the middle, to allow water to run off. If the yellow gravel mixed with clay, that forms such nice walks, cannot be obtained, any other gravel, mixed with road scrapings, will answer, though it will not look so well. No walk, be the garden ever so small, should be less than three feet wide. Box, the neatest of all edgings, should now be planted; a foot in length of old edging will make several yards of new. Take the old box and divide it into small pieces, each having root fibres; trim the tops. Stretch a line tight along the ground exactly where you intend the edging to be; with the spade open a small trench along the line, the side of the trench next the walk being perpendicular; place the pieces of box along the perpendicular side of the trench, keeping their tops level; fill the earth into the trench, and press it well down with your foot—giving water. Dig and prepare the ground for next month: you cannot turn it over too much.

GARDENING FOR MARCH.

FLOWER GARDEN.

HARDY annuals may be sown from the second week to the end of the month. The weather being fair, the ground well dug, finely raked, and not too wet, sow in circular patches, dropping from six to eight of the larger seeds, and from fifteen to twenty of the smaller kinds, in their respective patches, covering them with not more than from a quarter to half an inch of earth, according to the size of the seeds. Do not too finely pulverize the soil you cover with, if you do, the first shower will dissolve it to mud, and the next sunshiny day bake it into an impervious cake. Sow first the seeds of the tallest growing-kinds at the farthest side of the border, or if in a bed, at the centre; then the next in

height, and so proceed, keeping the plants of least stature
next the walk. (We may here observe, that with all kinds
of plants this rule should be strictly adhered to.) Trample
the ground as little as possible, and when finished sowing,
efface any footmarks with the rake. Remember to leave
space for the more tender annuals and other plants that you
may wish to sow or plant out next month. When the young
plants appear above ground, they should be thinned, picking
out the weakest and most crowded; and again, as they
advance, be subsequently thinned at intervals, until not
more than three, four, five, or six plants, according to their
size, are left in each patch. Stir the soil about them frequently, and water and stake when necessary. Many persons
who have the space, sow their annuals in a reserve garden,
transplanting them when they have made four or five leaves,
to the places where they are to flower. This is generally
considered to be the best plan, for transplanting checks
over-luxuriance in the stems and leaves, causing new root-
fibres to be formed, which supply nourishment for the
development of flowers. However, those annuals which
have few fibrous roots, such as Poppies, Lupins, Mignionette,
Sweet Peas, and others, cannot bear transplanting, and consequently must be sown where it is intended they are to
remain. The object of growing annuals not being to produce
shoots and foliage, but an abundance of fine flowers, they
should not be sown in a very rich soil. For the same reason
they should always be grown in an open situation, exposed
as much as possible to the solar ray. Like most herbaceous
plants, the bloom of annuals may be greatly prolonged, by
plucking off the flowers as they fade, thereby not permitting
them to produce seed. Many annuals, thus treated, will
continue to flower, adding beauty to the autumnal garden,
until they are destroyed by winter's frost.

A few of the finest plants, however, ought to be permitted
to bear seed for next year's use. Never sow the seeds of
plants that produce flowers of the same colour next each

other, but endeavour to contrast them as much as possible.
Blue and orange, red and blue, yellow and rose, orange and
violet, look well together; a sprinkling of white adding
effect to the whole. A list of hardy annuals would fill our
entire space, but any seedsman will, on application, furnish
you with a catalogue. We will just recommend a few,
naming their height and colour:—

From 2 to 3 feet high.—Golden Bartonia, orange; Larkspur, blue; Rosy Lupin, rose; Malope grandiflora, purple.

One foot in height.—Pretty Clarkia, white and pink;
Nemophilla insignis, blue; Viscaria oculata, pink with
dark eye.

Less than a foot in height.—Collinsia bicolor, white and
lilac; Leptosiphon Androsacea, rosy lilac; Kanlfussia
Amelloides, blue.

Do not forget, however, the good old annuals, the Mignionette, the Sweet Pea, the Ten-Week Stock, and Minor Convolvulus. The gay and useful Nasturtium should be sown,
after steeping the seeds a few hours in water, by palings,
back-walls, &c., where it can be trained in luxuriant
beauty.

Leave some space for the climbing annuals.

Window Gardening.

In the early part of this month, if the weather is fine, the
plants should be taken from their winter quarters; all dust
and decayed leaves carefully brushed and picked off; and
the more hardy plants, which have been in a window during
winter, may now be put out of doors, on warm days, to
enjoy a few hours' fresh air and sunshine, or a little warm
gentle rain; removing them to their old quarters on the
approach of evening. Preparations must be made for spring
potting, which should be performed about the middle of the
month. Water the plants two days previous to potting, so
as to have their soil in a moist state, neither wet nor dry;
and, if possible, have your fresh compost in the same con-

dition. If you use new pots, let them be exposed to the atmosphere, or soaked in water; and if you use pots that have held plants, let them be well washed before potting. Good drainage, and using pots suitable to the dimensions of the roots, are the chief objects to be attended to. For drainage, place an oyster-shell or rounded piece of potsherd over the hole in the bottom of the pot, and over that pieces of potsherd, bricks, tiles, or cinders, about half an inch square, to the depth of an inch, the smallest pieces uppermost. Now take the plant that is to be re-potted, turn it upside down, with your left hand across the mouth of the pot, the stem of the plant being between your fingers; give the edge of the pot a few taps on any solid substance, lift up the pot as you would an extinguisher from a candle, and you have the plant and ball of earth in your left hand. Examine carefully the ball of earth; if it is full of healthy roots, the plant requires a pot one size larger than that which you have just taken it from. Take a drained pot of that size, and lay just as much soil over the drainage as will raise the surface of the ball of earth to three-quarters of an inch from the top of the pot; place the ball and plant in the centre of the pot, and fill up all round the sides with fresh soil, pushing it firmly down with a small flat stick; cover the ball to the depth of a quarter of an inch, thereby leaving a vacant space of half an inch at the top of the pot for the purpose of supplying water; strike the bottom of the pot flatly two or three taps on a solid substance, water the plant, and place it in the shade for a few days till established. Thus you will understand that the healthy, abundantly-rooted plant, requires a pot one size larger. On the other hand, should you observe, when you turn the plant out, that its outside roots are decayed, that the ball of earth is poor, dry, and gritty, then you should gently remove the decayed roots and barren soil, and put the plant in a pot of the same size as the one you have taken it from. Again, you may find the plant injured by imperfect drainage, or injudicious watering;

in that case, take away as much of the soddened soil and rotted roots as you can, and put the plant in a much smaller pot, with a light soil, watering sparingly until the appearance of the foliage denotes the re-establishment of the plant's health. Sometimes, especially with Scarlet Geraniums, you will find a large brown root coiled up in the pot, like a sleeping centipede; cut it off close to the main root, (fresh, more healthy, more nourishing roots will speedily grow in its place), and put the plant in a pot of the same or a smaller size. The piece of root taken off, if cut into three-inch lengths, planted in a pot of sandy soil, a quarter of an inch of each length uncovered, and kept moist and warm, each piece will grow, producing fine young plants.

Never pot a plant that has its ball of earth quite dry, for you cannot give it water afterwards; all the water you may administer will run down the fresh soil at the sides of the pot—the plant experiencing the fate of Tantalus. Never place plants in pots in the open air, without having boards, tiles, slates, coal-ashes, or similar materials, beneath them, to prevent their being entered by worms, or the holes in the bottoms being clogged with soil. Sow annuals in pots. The Nemophilla insignis, Brachycome iberidifolia, Rhodanthe Manglesii, Lobelia gracilis, from their beauty and low growth, are peculiarly applicable for window annuals; the last-named has an excellent effect, if suspended by a wire or cord from the top of the window, besides giving oom for another pot on the sill.

KITCHEN GARDEN.

Now sow *Lettuces* immediately, broad-cast, in a light, well-manured soil, and open situation; rake in lightly. When the plants attain about three inches in height, thin out, planting as many of the thinnings as you require, or have room for, twelve inches apart, in beds. Keep thinning, by gathering for use those that remain in the seed-bed, or transplant as above directed. Water freely when transplanting, and hoe and water the thinned seed-bed. When the Cos Lettuce is about three parts grown, it may be forwarded in cabbaging by tying the leaves moderately close together with a string of bass. For a seed-bed three feet broad, and eight feet long, one-eighth of an ounce of seed will be sufficient, and should produce about two hundred plants. One plant permitted to stand will produce abundance of seed, which must be carefully gathered as it ripens, else, being very light, it will be blown away.

Sow *Onions.*—To attain a good size, they require a rich mellow ground, on a dry subsoil, and an open situation : none but thoroughly rotten manure should be used. Sow broad-cast, and moderately thick, in beds about four feet wide, raking the seed in lengthways : after sowing, tread the surface of the bed down firmly. When the young onions are three inches high, weed carefully, and thin to about three inches apart ; as they advance, thin to five, six, or seven inches apart, according to their size. If there are any vacant spots in the bed, caused by the failure of the seed, fill them up with the thinnings. Keep the bed free from weeds, and water freely when requisite. When the leaves begin to die at their points, and turn yellow, lay the stems down close to the ground, bending them about two inches up the neck ; this promotes the ripening of the bulb. When the necks shrivel, and the leaves decay, pull up the onions, and spread them out in the sun, on a gravel walk or dry piece of ground ; turn them every two or three days, and in a week or a fortnight they will be ready to house. Then clear off the leaves, stalks, and fibres ; lay them in a dry room, turn them over occasionally, picking out any that decay, and they will keep sound till the month of May. For a bed four feet broad, and twelve feet long, an ounce of seed is enough, if the plants are to be drawn young ; but if it is intended they are to grow to maturity, half an ounce of seed will be sufficient.

Sow *Parsnips.*—The soil for parsnips should be light, free

from stones, and dug or trenched at least two spits deep; the manure should be perfectly decomposed, or if recent, dug into the bottom of the trench. Sow broad-cast or in drills, moderately thin, and rake the seed lengthwise well into the ground; when the plants are two or three inches high, weed and thin them to from nine to twelve inches apart. Keep them afterwards free from weeds, till the leaves cover the ground, after which no future culture is required. About the end of October, the decay of the leaf will indicate the maturity of the root. To save seed, transplant some of the best roots in February, inserting them over the crowns; they will soon shoot up in strong stalks, and produce large umbels of seed, ripening in autumn. For a bed five feet by twenty, half an ounce of seed is the usual proportion.

Sow *Carrots*.—The carrot requires a light, mellow, sandy soil, which should be dug or trenched two spits deep, breaking all the lumps, so as to form a porous bed, and an even surface. Previous to sowing, the seeds should be mixed with sand or ashes, and rubbed between the hands, in order to separate them as much as possible. Sow on a calm day, and tread in well before raking. When the plants are two or three inches high, weed and thin from three to five inches apart such as you intend to use when young or half-grown—but the main crop that you intend to produce full-size roots thin to eight inches asunder. A quarter of an ounce of seed is sufficient for a bed three feet wide and eleven feet long.

Sow *Parsley* in shallow drills, to form an edging where convenient. When the plants come up they should be thinned to four or six inches apart. As the curled kind is considered to be the best, be careful when thinning to pick out the smooth-leaved plants. Parsley will grow well in shady situations, where few other plants would thrive.

Plant *Horse-radish* in the beginning of the month. Trench the ground eighteen inches deep: if you apply manure, be careful to let it be only in the bottom of the trench. Make holes in the trenched ground, eighteen inches apart every way, and sixteen inches deep. Take a root of horse-radish, cut off the extreme top, then cut the rest of the root into pieces an inch and a half in length; drop a piece into each hole, and fill it up to the surface with fine sifted cinder-dust; rake even, and keep free from weeds.

Plant *Shalots.*—Divide the roots into their separate parts called cloves, and plant by merely pressing each clove slightly into the soil, leaving their tops uncovered; they require no more attention than merely keeping the ground clear of weeds, and when the leaves have attained their full size, tying them together in knots, which will facilitate the ripening of the bulbs. In autumn, when the leaves are decayed, take up, and preserve, as onions.

Plant pieces of the roots of *Jerusalem Artichokes* in drills three feet apart, and two feet between the sets, covering with three inches of earth. As they grow from seven to eleven feet high, they form excellent screens for hiding any unsightly object; for the same reason they should not be planted where they will shade other crops.

GARDENING FOR APRIL.

FLOWER GARDEN.

THE seeds of perennial and biennial flowering plants should now be sown. Perennials are those plants which produce flowers and seeds for an indefinite period of time. Though trees and shrubs are, strictly speaking, perennials, yet the term is more particularly applied to plants of herbaceous habits, whose stems, leaves, and flowers annually decay at the approach of winter, the roots retaining the vital principle, and reproducing the perfect plant the following season. Most perennials thrive best in a light and rather rich loamy soil; it should not be too rich, else they will grow too strong, consequently producing but few flowers; neither ought it to be too poor, for then no part of the plant will grow to perfection. Perennials will grow under the shade of trees and bushes, but they will flower much finer and better if planted in a more open situation. Sow in well-dug and finely-raked beds, covering lightly, according to the size of the seed. As soon as the young plants have formed three or four leaves they should be thinned, and the thinnings transplanted into another bed. Transplant once or twice, according to the strength or weakness of the plants; your object being to bring them on as far as possible the first season, without permitting them to flower; early in the ensuing spring they must be planted out where they are intended to remain. The Scarlet Lychnis, Sweet William, Columbine, Antirrhinum or Snap-dragon, Perennial Larkspur, Perennial Lupin, Late-flowering Starwort, Everlasting Pea, and Wallflower, are all old and deserving favourites in this class of plants. Some of the less hardy perennials, as the different kinds of Mimulus (Monkey or Cardinal flower), Pentstemon, Salvia, &c., require in winter to have their roots sheltered with litter or coal ashes; by using this precaution, you need lose scarcely one of these plants during the severe frosts of winter. The Wallflower, as its name implies, grows well upon the top of a wall, not too much exposed to the sun; all that is required being merely to place a few seeds and a little earth on the wall. The Thrift, or Sea-Pink (*Armeria Maritima*), whose natural habitat is barren rocks on the sea-coast—many varieties of the Sedum or Stonecrop—many varieties of Fern, or the London Pride, all these will grow upon walls, greatly adding, not only to the beauty, but even to the extent of a small garden. The seed of the Marvel of Peru, one of the choicest ornaments of the garden, and not half so generally cultivated as its beauty deserves, should now be sown. Though it does best in a hotbed, yet it can be successfully grown by sowing in pots kept in a warm room. By June, or perhaps earlier, the young plants may be turned out into a sunny border of the garden : during the time they are in flower, if the weather is dry, they should be watered twice a day ; this will increase the size and keep up a succession of the flowers till the buds are killed by the frost. The stems should then be cut down, and in a few days after the roots lifted and laid in dry sand, or hung up in a paper-bag in a dry place till the spring ; being then potted, and kept in a warm room, they will soon shoot forth, and about the middle of May may be turned out again into the open border. The best compost for the Marvel of Peru is a mixture of cowdung and ashes with common mould. Now is the time for dividing and planting the roots of that universal favourite the Dahlia. Propagating by. dividing their tubers is the easiest method of increasing your store of these plants. Examine each root carefully, rejecting any that are unsound ; if only a small part of the root is decayed, cut it out. Then cut them into as many pieces as will permit you to have, at least, one eye and a good-sized bit of root in each part. If you have the advantage of a hotbed, the roots should be laid on it for a few days previous to dividing them ; this will cause the eyes to push, and consequently you will be better able to discern where and how you ought to cut. Pot each piece singly, and keep the pots in a warm place until the plants are fit to be turned out into the open ground. A still safer mode is to plant the roots whole, towards the end of the month, in a warm open border, about an inch below the surface, covering them with a light loose soil. If any frost occurs, a little litter should be thrown over them at night. When the shoots have grown an inch above the soil, either take up the roots, or else scrape the soil carefully from around them, and cut them into as many parts as there are shoots, being careful that a good bit of tuber is attached to each. Plant these divisions separately in the places where you intend them to flower. Immediately that you see the plant is established, it should be staked. Give water when required, and if the summer

be very dry, a covering of moist dung round the base of
their stems will be of great benefit to the plants. As they
advance, tie the stems rather loosely to their respective
stakes. On the first appearance of frost, cut down the stems
to within a few inches of the ground, and a few days after,
lift the roots dry, and store them away in a dry place till
spring. Earwigs are most destructive to the Dahlia. Small
tubular traps should be hung about the flowers and stakes;
these traps must be examined several times a day, and the
enemy, when caught, ruthlessly destroyed.

Biennials are plants which, like annuals, generally die
after producing their flowers and seeds, but are usually two
years in perfecting these, and in some instances may be in-
duced to flower for two or three successive seasons by pre-
venting them from maturing their seed; their general
culture and management is the same as for perennials. One
of our most deservedly popular biennials is the Stock July
flower, or, as it is more generally termed, simply the Stock.
The seed should be sown in the first week in April, in a
warm spot of ground open to the south-east, and sheltered
from cold winds. The bed being well dug, raked, and
levelled, scatter in the seeds, sifting over them a quarter
of an inch of fine mould. When the plants appear they
must be thinned where too thick, and carefully and re-
peatedly watered. In the latter end of May, prepare another
bed in a similar manner and situation as the former, and
shift the young plants into it from the seed-bed, placing
them about five inches apart every way: when all are
planted, give them a gentle watering, repeating it morning
and evening till they are rooted; after that you may only
water once in every three days till the end of August. At
that time let a large bed be made for them in the flower
garden, and let the plants be taken up in the evening of a
cloudy day, and planted in it at two feet distance. Here
they will flower the ensuing summer, and there will be
amongst the lot some common single kinds, some semi-

double, and some very fine double ones. Pull the common ones up as soon as their flowers open, so as to distinguish them; this will give more room for the others. The finest single plants, such as show a tendency to doubleness by having a few more than their proper number of petals, say five, six, or seven, should be selected to save seed from. Any particularly fine plant may be propagated by slips or cuttings, but they will not flower so well as those raised from seed; and where a good quantity of judiciously-selected seed is annually sown, there will always be plenty of double flowers.

Sow Annuals to succeed those sown last month. The China-aster, one of our finest autumnal flowering annuals, should now be sown. To grow it to perfection, select a piece of ground for your seed-bed, open to the sun, and sheltered from cold winds; sow thinly, and when the seedlings are about three inches high, prepare another bed in a similar situation, by digging a spade deep, and breaking the mould fine. Transplant to the latter bed in the evening of a cloudy day, taking up each plant with as much mould as possible adhering to its roots; plant them in holes, about six inches apart, previously opened in the new bed for their reception, and give a moderate watering. Shelter from the sun and wind, and if the weather is dry, water every evening, till the young plants are well rooted. Break the soil about them with a hoe every few days, and if any of them appear blighted, cut off the injured part. In about six weeks they will be fit for removing to where they are to flower.

The Asters show to the best advantage in a bed, and not dispersed among other plants in the borders. Let, then, a bed be dug two spades deep, mark it with lines lengthways and across, from one foot and a half to two feet apart; and in the centre of each square formed by the intersecting lines open a good-sized hole; holes also should be opened in different parts of the borders. In showery weather, or a cloudy evening, take up the plants with a large ball of mould attached to each. The strongest and healthiest should be planted in the bed, one in every hole; shading and watering as before. The inferior or weaker plants may be put in the holes in the borders. They must now be watered frequently, and about every ten days break the earth about them to the depth of two inches. When they come in to flower, select the best plants for seed; from the others all flowers should be picked off as soon as they begin to fade; by these means, and good watering, you will keep the plants in beauty till the frost.

Sow climbing Annuals—all spare spaces of wall should be covered. The Nasturtium, Convolvulus Major, and Canary Creeper, are hardy annuals, suitable for this purpose. They should be sown immediately, and afterwards trained up strings attached to the wall, in the same manner as described for Scarlet Runners. Look over your Roses, and most probably you will find in many of the buds a small grub; this "worm i' the bud" must be picked out and destroyed. If your Roses are much infested by aphides, a washing with tobacco-water will be of service.

Window Gardening.

Give your plants as much light and air as you can, watering when requisite. If you have had any Scarlet Geraniums hanging up by their roots in a dark closet or cellar during the winter—an excellent plan, which we shall not forget when we have occasion to describe the best modes of wintering window-plants;—they may now be potted and kept in a warm room to give them a start previous to turning them out next month into the open ground.

Balsams may be easily raised in the window of a room wherein a fire is kept. Sow immediately in well-drained pots and a light rich soil, the seeds about an inch apart, and not more than a quarter of an inch in depth. When the young plants are about two inches high, pot them off separately into small pots with a compost of half-leaf mould, or thoroughly rotten dung and loam. As they advance they will require to be frequently shifted into larger pots, using pots of only one size larger each shift, and not putting them into large pots at once. Keep them as near as possible to the glass, and if they are in a side light, turn them daily. They require plenty of water, and in fine weather should be set out in the open air for a few hours in the middle of the day. Water should also be frequently applied over their leaves and branches, with a fine-rosed watering-pot. In summer you may either turn them out into the open ground, or retain them in the pots. The Balsam is what gardeners term a "rank feeder," thriving and flourishing upon quantities of liquid manure that would kill most other plants.

The formation of the Mignionette Tree should be commenced this month. It is a very interesting operation, and one peculiarly suitable for lady window-gardeners from the neat and careful superintendence it requires, as well as the singularity, beauty, and fragrance of the plant. We use the word *formation* advisedly; for though some botanists say that the Tree Mignionette (*Reseda odorata erecta*, they term it) is a distinct variety from the common Mignionette (*Reseda odorata*), yet we are perfectly satisfied, by practical experience, that the Tree Mignionette (or *erecta*) is merely the common garden Mignionette *formed* into the tree-shape by culture and training. We also, therefore, prefer to call the trained plant the Mignionette Tree. The process is as follows:—Sow five or six seeds of the common mignionette in and about the centre of a three-inch pot—observe that you will only have one *tree* from these seeds, and therefore you must employ as many pots as you wish to have plants. The soil should be rather rich, but not too heavy. When the plants come up, thin out the weakest successively, so as to leave only one of the strongest, and if practicable, the most centrally situated in the pot. Put a neat stick, or what is better, a stiff piece of wire, down by the side of the plant, pushing it down firm. When the plant is two inches high, commence tying it loosely with a worsted thread to the stick or wire, and keep tying it regularly as it advances. Every side-branch that appears from the main stem must be pinched off; but the leaves must be allowed to remain on the stem, as their functions are necessary for the support and strength of the plant. During the summer, when the first pots are full of roots, the plants should be shifted to pots one size larger. When the plants have attained the height of a foot or more, according to the fancy of the cultivator, the side-shoots must be permitted to extend themselves from the top, but must occasionally have their ends pinched off, to force them to form a bushy head of ten or twelve iches in diameter. About October this will be accomplished, and the head in full bloom and fragrance ; one plant will sufficiently scent a large drawing-room. Next season a side-shoot must be substituted for the previous leader, and the plants shifted into larger pots, if they require it. With care these *trees* will last for several years.

KITCHEN GARDEN.

Sow Celery in the early part of the month. Sow in a bed, in some warm, rich corner of the garden—a border with a southern aspect is to be preferred ; rake in the seed lightly and regularly. If the weather is dry, give moderate watering both before and after the plants come up. When they are two, three, and four inches high, thin the seed-bed by pricking out a quantity at successive times into intermediate beds, which have previously been well dug, raked and rolled, or beaten down with the back of a spade. Place the young plants about four inches apart ; water, and, if possible, shade from the sun during the heat of the day, until they have taken root. When the plants left in the seed-bed, or those removed to the intermediate bed, are six inches high, they must be transplanted into trenches for blanching. For this purpose, choose an open spot of ground.

Mark out the trenches a foot wide and three feet apart; dig out each trench lengthwise, a spade in width, and about six or eight inches in depth. Lay the excavated earth in the intervals between the trenches. Dig in about two or three inches thick of good well-rotted dung, and level the bottom of the trench. Then, having lifted the plants, cut off any long straggling tops from their leaves and root fibres; also slip off any side-shoots, and plant a single row in the bottom of each trench, six inches apart; water directly and frequently afterwards, till the renewed growth of the plants shows that they have taken root. As blanching depends on excluding the light, when the plants are about ten inches high, commence to lay up the earth in dry weather to the stems of the plants, adding more earth every week or ten days as the plants advance, always taking care to leave six or seven inches of the leaves above the surface of the soil. The soil used for earthing-up should be broken very fine, and placed along the edge of each row; then the stems and leaves of the plant ought to be collected together in one hand, while the soil is placed carefully about them with the other. This process, though troublesome, is necessary to prevent the soil from falling into the hearts of the plants, which invariably causing them to rot, stops their growth and renders them useless. When taking the crop, begin at one end of the row, and dig down to the roots, loosening them with the spade, so that the plants may be drawn up entire without breaking their stalks.

GARDENING FOR MAY.

FLOWER GARDEN.

You may still sow the seeds of hardy annuals, to succeed, in flowering, those sown last month; sow in the borders where they are intended to flower. Propagate by cuttings the double perennials and biennials that do not produce seed, such as double Stocks, double Wallflowers, Sweet Williams, Scarlet Lychnis, Phlox, Rockets, &c. Choose some of the best flower-stalks before they get too hard, cut them into lengths containing three or four joints each, take off the lower leaves, and plant the cuttings about four inches apart, in a bed previously prepared in a warm situation, the top joint or bud of the cutting above ground. They must be shaded from the sun until they have taken root. If covered with a bell or hand-glass, they will strike root with greater quickness and certainty; water the soil before inserting the cuttings, and press the glass down firmly over them, they will then scarcely require a further watering till they have rooted. Every tree, shrub, or plant that produces buds may be propagated by cuttings, each bud containing the germ of a new plant, and only requiring to be separated from the parent stem and treated *secundum artem*, to enable it to produce leaves, stems, flowers, and roots. It does not come within our limits to inquire, critically, whether this is the generation of a new plant, or merely the extension of an old one, but as there is a great deal of misunderstanding existing with respect to how the cutting is furnished with roots, we give the following explanation from Loudon:— "If the trunk of a tree is lopped, and all its existing buds destroyed, then there will be protruded from between the wood and bark a sort of protuberant lip or ring formed from the proper juice, and from which there will spring a number of young shoots. The formation of the root in the case of the slip (cutting) is effected in the same manner, the moisture of the soil encouraging the protusion of buds at and near the section, and the bud that would have been converted into a branch above ground is converted into a root below." Cuttings should be taken from the young and newly-formed woody part of the plant, but the lower extremity of the cutting should not be too young and soft, lest it absorb too much moisture and rot; neither should it be too old and hard, for then it will not be able to imbibe as much moisture as will enable it to root and grow. Consequently cuttings should be taken off at the junction of the old and new wood, by which either of the extremes will be avoided. Cuttings should also be taken off just below a bud, as they only form roots from buds, and if a bud is not left at the base it is liable to rot; the cut should be made smoothly and horizontally across the stem, taking care not to bruise the bark nor leave it jagged. Most hardy, hard-wooded shrubs and plants, are easily propagated by cuttings planted in the open air; but tender, herbaceous, and watery-stemmed plants require more care, and should be covered with a bell or hand-glass, or kept in the window of a warm room. A certain degree of heat, shade, and moisture is requisite to enable cuttings to strike root. They should, therefore, if inserted in the open ground, have a warm situation; and as too much moisture is as fatal as too little, a light soil; if planted in pots, good drainage. Shade is necessary, because an exposure to the sun or strong light evaporates the little moisture the cuttings retain, causing them to wither and die. Therefore the cuttings should be shaded by a piece of mat placed over the hand-glass, or if in the open ground, a few willows may be hooked over them to afford a similar shelter. All the leaves, except two or three at the top, and any flower-buds, should be carefully trimmed off the cutting before it is planted.*

Towards the end of the month, tender annuals that have been raised in the house, and all window plants that you wish to turn out into the open borders, may be planted out. Geraniums, Fuchsias, Verbenas, Hydrangeas, and other similar plants, will grow and flower to greater advantage in

---

* An old lady, and an excellent gardener, *always inserts a grain of corn in the lower part of her cuttings, for the purpose of supplying them with roots!*

the open air during the summer than if retained in their pots, besides giving you more room in your windows. Be careful to give water when required, and for your own credit do not let a weed be seen.

Window Gardening.

One of the most popular of window plants is the Geranium, and its delicate scent, rich bloom, and pleasing foliage well merit the general estimation in which this beautiful flower is held. As a good deal of confusion exists in many minds with respect to what are geraniums and what are pelargoniums, I will endeavour, before I proceed further, to explain this distinction—one, indeed, now almost without a difference. The geranium, so named by Linnæus, from *geranos*, a crane, on account of the termination of the carpels bearing some fancied resemblance to the bill of that bird, is placed in the sixteenth class (*Monadelphia*) and sixth order (*Decandria*) of his system. Several species of the geranium are natives of this country, their flowers, though small, being very beautiful; the herb Robert, a common British plant, is a familiar type of the species. The finer kinds of geranium, however, have been introduced from abroad, and naturalized in our windows and greenhouses. The pelargoniums are all strictly exotic; they are named from the fancied resemblance of their capsules to the bill and head of a stork, *pelargos.* They are placed in the same class of the Linnæan system as the geranium, but in the fourth order (*Heptandria*). In the natural system of botany both the geraniums and pelargoniums are included in the division *Dicotyledons* (plants with two or more cotyledons, or seed leaves), forming, with other plants of close affinity, the order *Geraniaceæ.* The geraniums and pelargoniums now cultivated have been so blended together by hybridization, that they are now universally known under the homely, good old-fashioned name, of geranium. I hope that the most of my readers have at least one of these gay plants in their windows; those who have not should procure one immediately: from that one they may make many, either for themselves or friends. The geranium is principally propagated by cuttings; and to grow it to advantage requires close pruning—the prunings are mostly used for cuttings. After the plant has done flowering, that is, when the first show of summer flowers has past, is the proper time to commence pruning and propagating. For a few days before and after pruning, the plants should have no water given to them; this prevents them from losing sap, or *bleeding*, when cut, and also enables the wounds to heal more quickly. The best geranium growers, those who produce the finest plants, prune closely, cutting the branches down to within three inches of the old wood, the growth of last season. After pruning, keep the plants inside your window for a short time, till you see the young buds commence to develop their leaves; you may then put them out in a warm sheltered corner till the end of autumn. Some gardeners pursue another plan when they prune; they also turn the plants out of their pots, shake the soil away from them, and cut away all the large roots to within four or five inches of the stem, at the same time shortening the lesser ones; the plant is then re-potted in a smaller pot—one, in fact, just large enough to hold the remaining roots without cramping them. After this severe operation of root and branch pruning, the plants should be kept in a close warm window, and shaded from the sun for about a fortnight. By that time they will be quite convalescent; fresh, vigorous root-fibres will rapidly form, speedily filling the small pots; so that in about another six weeks the plants will require to be re-potted back to their old pots; in these last pots they are intended to flower. At the re-potting for flowering, whether it be in autumn or spring, a slight sprinkling of bone-dust, or if that cannot be procured, some thoroughly rotted manure, should be laid over the drainage in the bottom of the pot. In my directions for March I

have given full instructions for potting, and I have so frequently spoken of the great importance of drainage, that I
shall say no more on that subject. Under this system of
management the plants should not be laid up dry, but kept
in a window, or in a cold room, pit, or frame, through the
winter. Now, suppose that you have half-a-dozen plants,
of course you would wish that they should not all be in
flower at once; so, to have them flowering in succession,
if the plants are kept in a window, cut off an inch or two
from the tops of the leading shoots of two of the plants
about the end of January—this will throw them back so
that they will not flower until two other plants, that you
must not cut, are going out of bloom; again, about the end
of February, cut the remaining two—these will succeed those
out in January. If the plants are kept in a cold room or
frame, bring a couple into the window of a warm room in
February, this will start them; in another month bring in
two more; to be succeeded by the remainder. During the
spring the plants should be watered when requisite, but no
liquid manure given until the flower-buds appear, then it
may freely be applied twice a week with great care; the
danger in applying liquid manure is giving it too strong, it
ought always to be well diluted with water. The slops of the
wash-hand bason are always handy, and may be applied
daily as pure water, with a better effect. When the stalk
bearing the flower-buds is well extended from the foliage,
and the branch from whence it arises has grown a joint or
two above the place where the flower-stem joins it, the top
of the branch should be pinched off, thus throwing the
strength of the plant to the formation of the flowers.

Another excellent method of managing geraniums, and
particularly applicable for those who, like the majority of
window gardeners, are pinched for room, is, in this month,
when all danger from frost is over, to turn out the plants
from the pots into the open garden. A well-dug spot of
light loamy soil, mixed with a little thoroughly rotten

manure, being most suitable for them: here they will grow luxuriantly, and should be permitted to flower all the summer. Early in the autumn cuttings should be taken from them, and these, when rooted, potted off into small pots—one in each, and kept as much as possible in the open air, till winter requires that they should be taken in to the window of a warm room, and there kept till spring, then to be planted out in the open garden as before. By this routine of management you always have an annual succession of young plants, which are generally the best bloomers. After taking the cuttings from the plants in the open air, you may either leave them to perish from the winter's frost, or you may take them up, and re-pot them, pruning close as before directed. An excellent and safe plan of wintering geraniums that have been growing in the open air, especially if they are of the large scarlet kind, is to take them up in the autumn, shake all the earth from their roots, and hang them up head downwards in a dark dry closet or cellar, where they will be safe from frost; in spring they should be planted out again in the open air, and though at this time they will have a very shabby appearance, they will immediately commence growing, vegetating rapidly, and flowering luxuriantly. Geranium cuttings should be taken from the healthiest plants, and inserted, without lacerating or bruising the bark at the base of the cutting, in well-drained pots, in a compost of loam and sand; the pots should be covered with a bell or hand-glass, or kept in a window or green-house. Indeed, in June or July, the cuttings will do very well in the open border, by attending to the directions given respecting cuttings, in the previous parts of this chapter.

KITCHEN GARDEN.

About the 24th of the month is the time to sow Cauliflower seed, for what the London market-gardeners term the Michaelmas crop. Sow good seed of last year's saving moderately thick, in a bed of light earth, and a free open situation; rake in the seed carefully, and give water in dry weather. In June, or when the young plants have two or three leaves an inch broad, they should be pricked out into an intermediate bed, there to gain strength for their final transplantation. By the latter end of July they may be planted out about two and a-half feet asunder. Give water freely at each transplanting, until the plants have taken root. They will begin to produce heads in October, and will be in full perfection in November, and even December, if the weather is mild. Half an ounce of seed is sufficient for a seed-bed four feet and a-half wide and ten feet long. The soil for the seed-bed may be light, but for final transplant-ing can scarcely be too rich. Cleanings of stables, streets, cesspools, &c., ought, therefore, to be liberally supplied when large heads are required. Brocoli may be sown about the 20th of the month. Sow in a bed of rich soil; if the weather be dry, water the bed the evening before sowing. When the plants have five or six leaves rather more than an inch in breadth, they should be pricked out four or five inches apart into an intermediate bed, where they should have four or five weeks' growth, when they may be finally transplanted. Water carefully and frequently after trans-planting. The best sorts to sow now are the Purple Cape, Green Cape, and Grainger's early Cauliflower brocoli. For a seed-bed four feet in breadth and ten in length, an ounce of seed is sufficient. Brocoli, as well as most other vege-tables, may be cultivated in a superior manner without transplanting. This method, however, from taking up much room, and interfering with a routine of crops, is unsuitable for a very small garden. Mr. M'Leod, the inventor or adopter of this plan, exhibited to the Horticultural Society a specimen of brocoli grown without transplanting. The head was compact and handsome, measuring two feet nine nches in circumference, and weighing, when divested of its leaves and stalk, three pounds; the largest of its leaves was two feet long. Mr. M'Leod's process is as follows :—In the end of May, having prepared the ground, he treads it firm, and by the assistance of a line sows his seeds in rows two feet apart, dropping three or four seeds into holes two feet distant from each other in the row. When the seeds vegetate, he destroys all but the strongest, which are protected from the fly by sprinkling a little soot over the ground ; as the plants advance, they are frequently flat-hoed until they bear their flowers; they are once earthed up during their growth. Mr. M'Leod adopts the same mode in the cultivation of spring-sown Cauliflowers and Lettuces, and almost all other vegetables, avoiding transplanting as much as possible.

GARDENING FOR JUNE.

I HOPE that many of my readers will this month enjoy the sweet fragrance and bright colours of flowers which have been cultivated by their own hands, thereby reaching a rich reward for their previous care. Lest any one should construe the word care in an unpleasant sense, I must observe that the word pastime in its place would be more appropriate. Gray, the poet, and also a skilful naturalist, has well observed, that the enjoyment of life depends on our *" having always something going forward."* Again he exclaims, *" Happy are they who can create a rose-tree or erect a honeysuckle !"* It is indeed this very " having always something going forward " that constitutes the chief part of the delight experienced by the amateur gardener, the beauty and scent of the flower produced forming the crowning gratification. There is a pride also, a pleasing pride, in walking out in the morning with a flower of one's own

growing sparkling in the button-hole! I have no doubt
but that some of my readers will condemn this feeling,
until I say that I mean an honest pride—the sort of
pride that prevents a man from entering a pothouse—
the sort of pride that keeps him from running in debt—
the sort of pride that urges our honest, humble country-
men and women to strive by efforts of body and soul
to escape the degradation of the workhouse! The creation
of a beautiful object is certainly "a great fact" to be
honestly and justly proud of,—such a pride as a Danby or a
Baillie might feel. Thank God! that though He has im-
parted to but a few the rare talent of fixing and perpetuating
on canvass or marble the ever-changing hues and forms of
nature, still, the meanest capacity can [produce original
forms, outvying the genius-directed labours of the palette,
brush, or chisel, or even the robe of Solomon, in all his
glory.

FLOWER GARDEN.

Tulip and Hyacinth roots should be taken from the ground
when their leaves are quite decayed, and not before. These
roots, or, properly speaking, bulbs, require to be annually
raised from the soil, and kept for about three months in a
dormant state. They are usually propagated by offsets,
which should be taken from the parent bulb at the time of
taking up the plants. They also can be multiplied by seed;
but as tulip-seed will not produce a flowering plant until
seven or eight years after sowing, this mode of propagation
is employed only by rich amateurs and speculative florists
for the purpose of obtaining new varieties. Bulbs are store-
houses of prepared pulp, laid up by the plant for its use
the following season; so that the larger and fuller the
bulb is, the better it may be expected to flower. For this
reason the seed-pod should be picked off when the plants
have flowered, as maturing the seed would partly exhaust
the energy of the plant; and as the leaves prepare the pulp

for maturing the bulb, the plants must not be lifted until they are decayed. Take up the bulbs on a dry day, and spread them out in the shade. When they are quite dry, and somewhat hardened, separate the offsets from the older bulbs, and put up each sort separately in bags or boxes, keeping them in a dry place until October or November, when they should be again planted.

The offsets, after being separated, should be treated in the same manner till autumn, and then planted in a bed by themselves in any sunny part of the garden; if they attempt to flower the first season, the bud should be picked off, thus throwing the strength of the plant to the maturing of the bulb; the next season they will flower well, and after that they may be treated exactly as the old plants. Hyacinths begin to decay almost before the bulb has been properly matured; to assist Nature, then, it is strongly recommended that the plants be taken up and laid horizontally in ridges —the bulbs covered with earth, the stem and leaves exposed to the air; in this position the leaves speedily decay, and the bulbs swell to full maturity.

Fritillarias, Crown Imperials, Narcissuses, Jonquils, and other bulbous plants, after flowering, may be taken up for the purpose of separating the offsets. Fritillarias will not bear to be kept out of the ground any length of time, and therefore should be planted again immediately. Indeed, excepting tulips and hyacinths, the dormant period of bulbs are so different, and so little known, that it is best to err on the safe side, taking as a general rule that weak bulbs should not be kept out of the ground for more than a few days only; stronger ones for about a month.

Tall-growing plants should be supplied with stakes. Nothing looks more unseemly and slovenly—even if the garden is well furnished with flowers, and in other respects kept trim—than the neglect of this useful precaution. The stakes should be straight, and strong enough to support the plants, and not so high by a few inches. Considerable taste and judgment can be exercised in staking plants effectively. The stake should always be put at the back of the plant, so as to be as much out of sight as possible. In some instances, where the plant has several stems, the stake should be placed in the middle, and the stems tied round it, not, however, in a bunch as we generally see, but each stem tied separately to the stake, care being taken to allow the leaves and flowers to hahg freely in their natural position. Verbenas, and other trailing plants, that in large gardens are usually pegged down to form beds, should, when in mixed borders and small gardens, be tied up to stakes. Place the stakes at distances from each other, according to the size and number of shoots of the plant, a stake for each shoot, tying the latter up carefully as they advance in growth, so that when the plant is in full growth and flower, the outspread shoots will appear to the best advantage.

Window Gardening.

Many of the plants of this department will now be in flower, some in the windows, others in the open air. Watering at this season, when requisite, must be duly and punctually performed. As many persons may be increasing their stock, I shall take leave to recommend a few to their notice, giving at the same time their proper mode of treatment.

The *Begonia Discolor* (commonly called the elephant's ear, or blood-leaf), is a plant easily managed, and ornamental in a window. As it requires to be kept in a perfectly dormant state throughout the winter, it takes up no window room in that part of the year so trying to the window gardener. As soon as its stem and leaves decay, it should have no more water that season, and be put away in a dry cupboard, cellar, under a bed—any place, in short, where it will be quite dry and safe from frost. Early in the ensuing spring the plant must be taken from its winter quarters, and re-potted in a rich loamy soil; after which it should be constantly and liberally watered through the summer, till the decay of the leaf announces that the period has arrived for the winter treatment already described.

Various species of the Cactus tribe are also very suitable for window plants, as they take up but little room, are not difficult to manage, and please the eye by the grotesqueness of their forms as well as by the richness of their flowers. They are what is termed *succulent* plants, and require no water during winter. I cannot help here remarking how wonderfully, and with what all-seeing wisdom, the organization of these plants is adapted to the purposes of nature! Natives mostly of tropical climates, and barren rocks and sands, their pores exist only in a rudimentary state, to open or shut as nature requires them; being constantly open during the rainy season of the year, closing and remaining closed during the dry season, the vital fluids are retained in the consolidated stem. Thus a store of nourishment is laid up in the plant, supporting it through the scorching heat of a tropical drought, and where all else is parched and barren; many of the species affording both food and drink to man and cattle. Now, we see why these plants should have no water in winter is, that they have a supply within themselves; the dampness of our climate causing any additional quantity infallibly to rot them. Cacti require a light and rich soil, equal portions of loam, peat, and leaf-mould, with an addition of silver-sand, more or less, according to the clayey or sandy quality of the loam employed. Some add lime rubbish, broken very fine, which I approve of; others mix with the soil bits of hearthstone, from the size of a pea to that of a hazel-nut. I mention peat in the soil for cacti, as it has been highly recommended to me by both oral and written testimony; though, from my own experience, I can safely say that it is not, by any means, an indispensable ingredient. The plants should be potted immediately after they have ceased flowering, or after the time at which they ought to have flowered: I prefer this mode, though some, with very plausible reasons, prefer potting in March. The pots should be small, and the soil firmly pressed down round the collar of the plant. Keep them during winter in the window of a warm room, commencing to give water in March. The best way of giving water at first, is to put a little of it luke-warm in the saucer, letting the plant suck it up. When the plants are in their growing state, they ought to be well supplied with water, sprinkling a little occasionally over the stems; or, what is still better, expose them to a warm, gentle shower. (All window plants should have such over-head watering frequently during summer.) Keep the cacti in a sunny window, as close to the light as possible, till their growing season is over; then they should be set out in a sunny exposed situation in the open air, and less liberally watered. Before frost occurs, which is certain death to these plants, they should be put back into the window, and kept dry till the following spring. No window gardener ought to be without cacti. Some of the species that are of a pendant habit, such as *Cereus flagelliformis* (vulgarly termed rat-tails), and *Cereus Mallisoni*, may be suspended from the top of the window by a wire or cord. Others of the smaller-growing kinds—as *Mamillaria stellata*, *Echino-cactus*, *Stapelia bufonis*—may be placed on a shelf fitted across the window at the central sash; thus a small collection of this very interesting tribe will not take up one inch of the space generally dedicated to other plants.

KITCHEN GARDEN.

About the end of the month, turnips should be sown for a main crop. The turnips grow best in a light, moderately rich, and well-broken soil. Sow in drills a foot and a half apart, covering the seed with about two inches of earth, treading it down lightly, and raking in the direction of the drill. When the plants appear, thin out successively, until at last they are nine inches apart, and carefully keep them free from weeds. If you can catch the opportunity, sow in wet weather; if not, water the soil before sowing.

I have abstained from giving any instructions for making hotbeds to grow cucumbers, melons, and for forcing purposes, being well aware that I could fill up my space with matter more generally useful to my readers. Those who can afford such luxuries, can also afford to pay a professional gardener to cultivate them, or at least to put themselves in the way of doing so. Besides, the formation of hotbeds, and the art of cultivating plants in them, can no more be taught by written rules than practical navigation can. However, I shall now proceed to give directions for growing cucumbers in the open air, this month being the time to commence.

In a warm border and rich soil, dug neatly even, draw lines at intervals of five or six feet; and in these lines mark stations three feet and a half apart. Take your trowel, and at each of the stations form shallow, circular, saucer-shaped cavities in the surface, ten or twelve inches in width, and about an inch deep in the centre. Then sow, in and about the middle of each cavity, eight or ten seeds, covering them with about half an inch of soil. When the plants come up, and begin to put forth the first rough leaves, thin out the weakest; leaving not more than four of the strongest and most promising-looking plants in each hole. Earth these up a little between and close round their stems; pressing them a little asunder, and giving water to settle the soil about them. As they advance in growth, train out the leading runners, and water carefully in dry weather three times a week; if the weather is very dry and hot, water every day. About the beginning of August the crop will be in full production, lasting till the middle or end of September. In the lot, you will have many fit for table use, though the majority will be fit only for pickling.

The American Cress (*Barbarea præcox*), though dignified by that transatlantic denomination, is a native of Britain, and a very useful winter salad, particularly in situations where the common water-cress cannot be obtained. It may

be sown now, thinly, in drills one foot asunder, or as an
edging; thinning the plants, when they come up, to about
nine inches apart. When the leaves are three inches long,
they are fit for use, picking them off as you would parsley.
One quarter-ounce of seed is sufficient for fifteen feet of drill.
When the plants are pretty strong, say about the middle of
August, cut back a portion, so as to have a supply of young
and tender leaves for winter use. By cutting back at three
separate periods, and sheltering in severe weather with a
few light twigs, so as not to interfere with the growth of
the plants, covering the twigs with fern or dry litter, a succession may be kept up until spring. The American cress
is a really useful and valuable plant in either large or small
gardens, though but little cultivated. The winter cress
(*Barbarea vulgaris*) is used and cultivated similar to the
American cress, but is not so valuable a plant: it was long
considered to be a variety of the latter, but the celebrated
botanist and horticulturist, Dr. P. Neill, Canonmills, Edinburgh, has proved it to be distinct.

GARDENING FOR JULY.

FLOWER GARDEN.

WATER, weed, train, stake, and tie up wherever requisite;
although you may have a goodly show of flowers, yet the
least untidiness will spoil the appearance of the whole.

Pressed by limited space, and the urgency of the spring
operations, I have, as yet, been unable to notice all of those
plants which are termed, *par excellence*, Florists' flowers. I
therefore now embrace the opportunity allowed me by the
less busy month of July, to treat of those—the brightest
jewels in the diadem of Flora. The taste for florists'
flowers in England, is, with good reason, generally supposed

to have been brought over from Flanders with our worsted manufactures, during the religious persecutions of Philip II. of Spain ; and the cruelty of the Duke of Alva, in 1567, was the occasion of our receiving through the Flemish weavers, who sought an asylum in this country, Gillyflowers, Carnations, and Provence Roses. Many of those weavers settled in and about the city of Norwich, long celebrated for its flowers and gardens. From Norwich the taste seems to have spread to other manufacturing localities—Spitalfields, Manchester, Bolton, &c. In Scotland, the taste for florists' flowers is supposed to have been introduced by the French Protestant weavers, who took refuge there from the impolitic bigotry of Louis XIV., and the persecutions following the revocation of the Edict of Nantes, in the latter part of the seventeenth century. Those refugees established themselves in a row of houses in the suburbs of Edinburgh, still known as *Picardy*-row, or place. The taste appears to have spread, with the apprentices of these men, to Glasgow, Paisley, Dunfermline, and other places—for in Scotland, as in England, wherever hand-loom weaving is carried on, the operatives are found to possess a taste for, and occupy their leisure time in, cultivating flowers.

Florists' flowers are, generally speaking, those that have been improved in form, colour, or size, or in all these three combined. They are, in fact, nearly all the productions of art ; having been raised, by high cultivation, from insignificant, beautyless plants. Anyone who compares the wild Heart's-ease, and the cultivated Pansy—the wild and cultivated Tulip—the single and double Pink and Carnation, &c., must be struck by the very great difference between the same species in its natural and its artifical state ; and consequently, florists' flowers are one of the most impressive proofs of man's skill and ingenuity which the vegetable kingdom can exhibit. Florists' flowers are, also, those which *sport*, as it is technically termed by gardeners ; or, in other words, those which produce new and distinct varieties when propagated by seed. For a long time, these universally admired varieties have been raised, and brought to perfection, principally by men in humble life.

Auriculas,

To be grown to perfection, should be in pots; they are propagated by seeds and offsets; the former when new varieties are required, the latter for multiplying and continuing choice kinds. The best time for dividing the roots, and taking off offsets, or rooted slips, is when the plant has done flowering, and ripening its seed. Plant the divisions and offsets separately, in small pots, and in a rich soil. Almost every choice auricula-grower has his own particular compost or soil to grow them in; and I am enabled to say that a great deal of quackery, and belief in *nostrums*, generally enters into the composition. I consider it not so much any peculiarity of soil, but care, attention, and perseverance, that grows fine auriculas. One-half thoroughly rotted dung, one-fourth turfy-loam, one-eighth peat or heath-mould, and the rest rotted leaves and river sand; the whole, well mixed, frequently turned over, and exposed to the preceding winter's frost, is the compost generally used by auricula-growers, and the finest I have ever seen were grown in it. At the time of taking away the offsets, and dividing the roots, the old plants should be re-potted and then placed in the shade, or in the frame where they are to pass the winter. They must be protected during winter, either in a cold frame, or other shelter. Wherever the pots are placed, boards, bricks, ashes, or similar materials, should be put beneath them to prevent worms from entering, or the hole at the bottom of the pot from being clogged with soil. In fine weather, in early spring, the plants should be well exposed to light and air; and about February the soil on the surface of the pot should be removed to about the depth of an inch, and its place supplied with fresh, rich compost. Liquid manure should, about this time, be given once a week, and if, when the plants begin to show flower, more than one flower-stem arises, the weakest should be removed. If the umbel, or flower-head, seems too crowded with buds, a few of the smallest should be carefully snipped out of the bunch with a small sharp pair of scissors. When in full flower, the plants should be kept in the shade, which will prolong their bloom; and after they have done flowering, they should be again potted, and treated as before. Auricula seed should be sown from about the middle of February to the middle of March. Sow in pots about six inches in diameter, and six in depth, having secured a good drainage by filling them half full of cinders. Cover the seeds very lightly, and place the pots in front of a conservatory, the window of a room, or a cool frame. If you cannot command those conveniences, place the pots in a sheltered situation—where they can only have the morning sun—in the open air, covering them with a hand-glass. The seed, and soil in which it is sown, must always be kept moist, but not too wet. The best way to apply water is by means of a clothes-brush dipped in soft water, and then held in the left hand with the hair side uppermost; by briskly drawing the right hand over the wet hair, the water will fly off in a contrary direction, and in particles almost as fine as dew. This is the very best plan for watering any small and delicate seeds. If the surface of the soil in the seed-pots becomes mouldy or mossy, it should be carefully stirred all over with a pin to the depth of about the thickness of a shilling. In from three to five weeks the young plants will appear; you must then admit air gradually, by tilting up one side of the hand-glass; and about May it can be removed altogether, and the seed-pots placed in the coolest and airiest spot in the garden, keeping the soil moist, and at the same time protecting them from heavy rain. As soon as the young plants have acquired six leaves they must be transplanted into pots, or boxes, the plants about two inches apart; and when they have grown so that their leaves nearly touch, they should be again

E

transplanted into other pots, or boxes, the plants at this time
being placed four inches asunder; in these last they are to
remain until they flower in the following spring, when the
best flowers should be marked for cultivating in pots, and
the inferior ones for growing in the borders. As soon as
they have done flowering, the best should be potted separately, and treated in every respect as before mentioned
for the old auriculas; the inferior ones may be planted at
once in the borders.

Note well—if any weakly young plants do not flower the
first year, nurse them carefully till the next; if they do not
flower then, give them a third trial, and your care and perseverance may very probably be richly rewarded, as it frequently happens—in strict accordance with vegetable physiology—that from such plants the finest blooming varieties
are obtained.

The Polyanthus is quite hardy, and seldom perishes in the
coldest or wettest seasons; indeed, it is less able to bear the
heat of summer than the cold of winter—it should, therefore,
always be planted in a shady border. Fine show varieties
should be cultivated in pots. Their whole culture is so
similar to that of the auricula that I need not dwell
upon it.

Carnations and Picotees (the latter a variety of the
former) are well-known favourites. Hogg, in his "Treatise,"
observes, that—" Of all the flowers that adorn the garden,
whether they charm the eye by their beauty, or regale the
sense of smell by their fragrance, the carnation may be
justly held to take first rank." The carnation is propagated
by seed and layers. The seed should be sown in May, in
pots filled with compost, and a little fine mould, barely
sufficient to cover it, sprinkled over the seed. As soon as
the young plants are three inches high they ought to be
planted out a foot apart, in a bed of rich garden-mould, and
defended from heavy rains and frost by hoops and mats:
they will in general blow the following summer. Layers

should be made when the plant is in full bloom. All the lower leaves on the stem intended to be layered should be cut off, so that none of the leaves may be buried in the soil when the shoot is fastened down. Enter a sharp knife a quarter of an inch below the joint to be layered, pass the blade upwards, precisely through the centre of the stem, to half an inch above the joint; withdraw your knife, and cut off smoothly the tip or end of the tongue thus formed. Then carefully bending down the shoot so as not to break it, fasten down the joint with a small hooked peg, and cover with not more than three quarters of an inch of fine mould. Keep the layers moist, and shaded from the sun, and in about three or four weeks they will have taken root; they may then be cut away from the parent plant with about half an inch of the stem which connects them, and potted-off into small pots, three or four plants being placed round the margin of each. The soil should be composed of three parts turfy loam, two parts well-rotted manure, and one part of river sand; a little lime is also a useful ingredient, it being so destructive to insects. This compost should be well incorporated by frequent turnings, and exposed to at least one winter's frost.

The fine show varieties are cultivated in pots. The plants should be potted in March, and kept in an open airy part of the garden, under an arch of hoops, so that, in frost, heavy rains, or cold easterly winds, mats can be laid over for their protection; but in favourable weather, the plants must always be open to the air. When the flower-stems are eight or nine inches high, it will be requisite to support them with sticks forced into the soil in the centre of the pot, to which the stems are to be loosely tied as they continue to advance in height. Amateurs flower choice carnations on stages, as they show to the best advantage thereon. The stage supporters should stand in pans filled with water, to prevent the access of that most destructive insect, the earwig. In winter, dotted carnations require the same treatment as auriculas. They ought never to be shut up close when wet, as in this state they are liable to be destroyed by mildew. In fine weather they should be allowed air and light as frequently as possible. If the surface of the soil in the pots becomes green, or seems to be too compact and adhesive, it must be carefully stirred to the depth of half an inch, and a little dry sand sprinkled over it. In March the plants should be re-potted, and the same routine of culture continued throughout the year.

Pinks are much hardier than carnations, as they can endure the winter of this climate out of doors. Though potting is necessary to cultivate to perfection the fine show varieties, yet the pink is generally considered to thrive best in the open air. They are propagated by pipings and seed. The pipings, or young shoots, should be taken off immediately previous to, or during, the time the plant is in flower, or, indeed, as soon as the young shoots are of sufficient length. Take the pipings off just below the second or third joint : cut the end smooth, and take off the lower circle of leaves ; plant them about half an inch deep, in a well-watered and shady border ; cover them with a bell or hand-glass, and do not permit the sun to shine upon them. The pipings should be placed firm in the soil, and watered when necessary. After ten days admit air to them, by tilting up the front of the glass with a brick or stone. As soon as they appear to have struck root, they should be gradually exposed to light and air, and then removed to the bed, border, or pots in which they are intended to flower. The compost, and the mode of raising from seed, are the same as for the carnation.

Window Gardening.

At this sultry period of the year, all potted plants require to be carefully and liberally supplied with water. Always apply the water to the surface of the soil, not permitting any to remain in the saucer underneath the pot. When window plants are carelessly allowed to become too dry, the earth

separates from the sides of the pot, and all the water you
may then give escapes through the vacuity thus formed,
without being of any benefit to the roots of the plants. The
best plan you can adopt, under such circumstances, is to
immerse the pot up to the rim in water for a few minutes,
then take it out and let the superfluous moisture drain off
before placing it again in your window. The continental
gardeners knead in a little tough plastic clay, impervious to
water, all round the inside rim of the pot, forming a bason-
shaped cavity in the centre. This is a most excellent plan,
especially with large plants; and I am surprised that it is
not more generally adopted in this country. If possible, at
this season of the year, do not have the plants directly facing
the south, as the heat of a July sun will, in spite of water,
injure the tender rootlets or spongioles of your plants.
Plants will also keep longer in bloom when shaded than if
they are exposed to the sun. Therefore a south-west aspect
during the heat of summer is the best. Never water plants
when the sun is shining warm upon them, if you do they
will very soon show the effects of such treatment—becoming
what gardeners term scorched, though the word "frozen"
would be more suitable, as it is the intense cold caused by
the rapid evaporation of the water that injures plants so
injudiciously treated—just on the same principle as ice is
formed in a red-hot crucible. Hydrangeas and fuchsias, at
this season, require water twice a-day. Although the fuchsia,
on its first introduction to this country, about sixty years ago,
was treated as a stove plant, it now scarcely comes under
the department of window gardening; as many of the species,
in sheltered gardens, live throughout the winter in the open air.
. Fuchsias delight in a rich loamy soil, mixed with
sand, leaf-mould, and rotten manure. They are easily
propagated by cuttings, and the very leaf, if properly
managed, will grow, forming a new plant. Their winter
treatment is very simple, as they may be put away dry
in any out-of-the-way place where frost cannot reach

them—some persons even burying them in the ground. About February, or March, they should be taken from their winter quarters and potted, trimming back their roots and branches; about May they should be re-potted in larger pots, (fuchsias thrive best in comparatively small pots,) or else turned out of their pots into the open ground. They show to great advantage as standards. This form is obtained by shortening the side-shoots of a young plant, and training the stem up a straight stick, gradually removing the side-shoots—commencing at the base—as the plant advances in height. They may also be trained up to a wall, or planted in beds. Fuchsias left in the open ground during winter, should be cut down when their branches are killed by the frost, and some litter, or coal-ashes, laid round them. If you cover the soil about their roots with tan, ashes, leaves, &c., for about six inches deep, and tie up together the branches, thatching them over with fern-leaves, straw, or mats, so as to keep out frost and wet, you may carry them through the winter without losing a single shoot.

KITCHEN GARDEN.

Cabbage Coleworts are valuable family plants, as they can be used in their different stages of growth, all through the autumn, winter, and spring. Procure seed of the early, quick-hearting, middle-sized kinds of cabbage, as the York, Battersea, Sugar-loaf, or Antwerp; for any of these sorts, that may not be used as coleworts—if they do not run to seed—will form cabbages early in the spring; and to prevent them running to seed you should not sow previous to the last week of this month, or the first week of August. However, if you have room, and wish for a constant succession, you should make two or three sowings—say one in the first fortnight, another towards the end of the month, and the last in the first week of August. Coleworts may be used as greens when their leaves are as broad as a man's hand; when further advanced, as greens with closing hearts; and lastly, when assuming the cabbage form. Sow in well-dug beds; if the weather be very dry, water previous to sowing, and before and after the plants appear. When the young plants have two or three leaves, if they are too thick in the seed-bed, thin out, transplanting the thinning into an intermediate bed. When these and the others in the seed-bed have several leaves two or three inches broad, transplant finally into rows a foot apart—the plants six inches apart in the row; and when you take for use, pull the alternate ones, leaving those a foot apart that have to grow the longest and the largest. In every spare spot in your garden you should dibble in one of these useful plants. Exterminate weeds; and give water when requisite. Always water after sunset, or very early in the morning. Except where there are seeds, or tender young plants, it is the much better plan to give the soil a good drenching at once, than tantalize it with frequent sprinklings.

GARDENING FOR AUGUST.

BUDDING, ETC.

IT is my pleasing duty this month to treat on the budding of roses—one of the most interesting of horticultural operations. By the tyro in gardening, budding is generally considered a mysterious affair, requiring great skill and dexterity of manipulation to perform successfully. If any of my friendly readers have such an idea, I beg of them to dismiss it from their minds immediately; for now is the time when the operation ought to be performed, and when they ought, by all means, to try to accomplish it. I know many, myself included, who never saw a rose or any other

tree or shrub budded, previously to their successfully doing
it themselves. If you have only two roses, if of different
kinds, I would advise you to bud the one on to the other,
and *vice versâ*; if you are successful, you can scarcely
imagine the pleasure you will experience. You can then
say the heart-gratifying words—" Alone I did it !" In the
course of my description you will read of a budding-knife,
and probably you may, very naturally, say to yourself,
" Why should I give half-a-crown for a budding-knife,
merely to bud one or two roses with ?" Quite right,
friend, say I—" but," as the old proverb says, " there are
always two roads to a well ;" and so I will tell you what I
use for a budding-knife. I have an old razor which, like
many other people, I keep in pretty good order, for the
purpose of—root pruning—easing my understanding—
chiropedising—pshaw ! I must be explicit, even if vulgar—
I mean, cutting my corns ! Now a razor, in that condition,
is as sharp, and towards the point has the same convexity of
blade as that which forms the useful peculiarity of the budding-knife. The handle of the budding-knife is made of
ivory or bone tapered off at the lower part, wedge fashion,
with as sharp an edge as the material will admit. Now, to
effect the purpose to which this handle is applied, I use the
handle of an old worn-out tooth-brush, which I have scraped
down to a similar sharp, smooth, wedge-shaped edge.
Thanks to the too prevalent, yet useful Mother of Invention,
my budding-tools cost me *nil*, and at the same time perfectly
answer my purpose :—

" Let not Ambition mock *our* humble *tools !*"

Budding is the insertion of a bud, taken from one tree,
into the bark of another; and, as in grafting, the operation
will not succeed unless the bud and the tree to which it is
united are varieties of the same species, or genera of the same
natural family. In fact, the only difference between graft-

ing and budding—the principle of each being the same—is that in the former a shoot, or, as it is technically termed, a scion, is inserted into the stock or stem that is grafted; and in the latter a bud, which is simply a scion in embryo. The latter part of June, the month of July, and on to the middle of August, is the best season for budding. When you perceive the buds well formed in the axilla of the leaf, that is, between the foot-stalk of the leaf and the stem, and when the bark of the stalk can be freely and easily raised from the wood, then you have a sure criterion that you may safely commence to bud.

Select a smooth part of the stock at the height you wish, and the side least exposed to the sun; with your budding-knife make a horizontal cut across the bark through to the wood, but no deeper; from the centre of this cross-cut make another of a similar kind, perpendicularly downwards, about an inch, or rather more, in length—these two cuts will be in the form of a T. Then proceed to take off the bud—or, as it is technically termed, the shield—first cutting off the leaf, but leaving a part of the leaf-stalk. The shield must be carefully sliced out of the stem at one cut. (Figures a and b represent the stem and shield after their separation.) A portion of the wood must be taken off with, and attached to, the shield; the greater part of this wood must be carefully picked out, but it is essential that a portion should be left at

the back of the bud—if you do not do so, but make a hole
through the shield at the eye, or root of the bud, you may
throw it away as useless. Then, with the handle of the
budding-knife, separate, and turn back the bark from the
stock on each side of the perpendicular cut (it will then
resemble figure *d*), and insert the shield close to the wood,
and between it and the turned-back bark. Cut off the top
part of the shield horizontally (in the direction of the dotted
line *c*), and fit the remaining upper part of the shield accurately, and closely, to the cross-cut in the stock—on this
close contact of the two barks the success of the operation
principally depends. You must now lay down the turned-
back bark over the shield, and with a worsted thread, or bit
of bass, bind it down, leaving the point of the bud clear.
(Figure *e* represents the bud in the stock previous to its being
bound.) A friend informs me that he uses common adhesive
plaster for binding, and that it answers admirably. If the
weather be very warm, a handful of damp moss should be
loosely tied over all, leaving, as before, the point of the bud
exposed. In about a month, or six weeks, the ties may be
removed; and to throw the whole strength of the plant into
the bud, all shoots must be cut off, and suckers, whenever
they make their appearance, carefully eradicated.

By budding you may produce several kinds of roses upon
the same plant. The more tender exotic roses would scarcely
exist in this country if they were not budded on our more
hardy kinds. Indeed, it is now generally acknowledged that
all roses bloom finer, and last longer, when budded on the
common wild rose. Budding is also extremely useful for
filling up the vacancies which so frequently occur in peach
and apricot trees, when trained to walls, by branches dying.
Variegated shrubs, as holly, &c., are propagated by budding
on the plain kinds.

FLOWER GARDEN.

The common white and orange Lilies, Martagons, Peonies, Fritillarias, Irises, and several other bulbous and tuberous-rooted plants, should not be permitted to remain longer than two or three years at farthest in the same spot of ground, as they greatly exhaust and impoverish the soil, and their increasing offsets require room. About this season of the year, when you see the stems decayed, the roots may b lifted, the offsets taken away, and the old roots planted again in fresh soil. Although the old roots may be kept for some time out of the ground, yet they will grow stronger, and produce finer flowers next season, if they are immediately planted again. The offsets should be planted in nursery beds until they produce flowers, when they may be removed to the borders. All bulbs intended to be moved should be raised from the ground just as their stems are decayed, for if they have any period of rest previous to lifting, they will form their new root-fibres, and also the bud or germ of next year's stem; and if the root is taken up after these are formed, the progress of Nature is impeded, and, consequently, the flowers of next season will be inferior—assuming the plant bears any, which, after such rude treatment, is very doubtful.

Large specimens of the Chinese Chrysanthemum, growing in the open ground, may now be layered to produce small, pet, potted plants for the window. Choose the strong central shoots for this purpose; and as the stems of these plants are extremely brittle, it is advisable to peg down the shoots their whole length along the ground, and only to notch or slightly twist the stem at the part to be layered, which should not be more than three or four inches from the end. A three-inch pot, filled with rich sandy loam, should be sunk rim-deep in the soil to receive each layer. Secure the layer in the pot with a hooked peg, or by tying it to a stick thrust firmly down into the soil. Cover the surface of the pot with moss, which, as well as the soil, must be kept constantly moist. About the middle or end of September, when the pot is full of roots, cut off the connection between the layer and the parent plant, and pot the layers in pots of one size larger, keeping them shaded for a few days. Chrysanthemums are gross feeders, and flourish luxuriantly when freely supplied with liquid manure; but as your object, in making these layers, is to produce small plants—dwarfs, in fact—you should not apply any stimulating liquid until the flower-buds appear, then you may apply it as often as every two days.

Some of the more hardy kinds of annuals may be sown in the last week of the month; sow thinly and in an open situation. Such as survive the winter will come into flower much earlier than any that you may sow in the ensuing spring. The Catchflys, Collinsias, Candytufts, Clarkias, Nemophillas, Eryssimum Peroffskianum, and Eschscholtzia, are suitable for this purpose.

Window Gardening.

The Oleander has been well described as a "gem amongst plants." It is a native of the East, and in the sacred and romantic land of Palestine is always found wherever rivers or water-courses invite its thirsty roots. The banks of the Jordan are clothed with this beauti-ful plant; it flowers at the "rising" of that river, being then partly immersed in water; yet it bears the extreme heat and baked soil of an eastern summer, when the rivers have shrunk into their narrowest compass. Knowing this, we have a guide to the cultivation of the Oleander. From the end of September until March it should receive no more water than will prevent the soil from being crumbly; and during the rest of the year the pot should be kept in a saucer, pan, or tub, according to its size, immersed to nearly half its depth of water. A strong, rich, turfy loam is the most suitable soil. When the plant has made its summer growth, it should be placed out of doors in a sunny situation, sheltered from the north. It is easily propagated by cuttings. During the spring or summer months, if the young shoots are cut off close under the fourth joint from their extremities, and the three lower leaves taken off close to, but without injuring, the bark of the stem, these will make the best cuttings; and the simplest and most interesting mode of rooting them is to put them in small bottles or phials containing rain-water, kept in the window of a warm room. The cuttings should not be immersed deeper in the water than half-way up to the next joint above its base. In a short time, tiny white roots will make their appearance, and when these are above half an inch long, remove the cutting to a small pot filled with a light sandy soil, gently adapting the soil to the tender rootlets. Keep moist, and shade the cutting until the firmness and colour of the leaves show that the roots have taken hold of the soil. Cuttings of Fuchsias, and many other plants, may be struck in water in a similar manner. But though water produces roots rapidly, yet it cannot sustain growth; so in all cases the plants should be removed to soil when the rootlets are from half an inch to a whole one in length.

The following excellent plan—I speak from experience—of obtaining dwarf Oleanders to flower in the succeeding spring, when barely a foot in height, I extract from the "Gardener and Practical Florist," pp. 291, 292, 1843.— "At any time during September and October prepare a quantity of two or three jointed cuttings by removing the lowest leaves, and making the heel of each, immediately under the joint, perfectly smooth. Place an inch layer of broken potsherds, as drainage, at the bottom of a pot six inches broad; upon that a coating of moss, then a compost soil consisting of one part reduced turfy loam, and three or four parts of heath mould. Press this mixture firmly into the pot, water it, and make as many holes in it close round the side of the pot as there are cuttings. Into each hole pour half an inch of white writing-sand, set a cutting upon the sand in the hole so deep that it be at least midway between joint and joint, then fill the holes with sand, and cover the entire surface of the soil with a half-inch layer of the same. Saturate the whole with water, and see that the cuttings are fixed and immovable without some effort; upon this close contact of plant and soil depends much of the future success. The pot of cuttings may be kept in a heat of from fifty to fifty-five degrees during winter, and many plants, as we have proved, will be found perfectly rooted in early spring. Among the cuttings taken from a full-headed strong plant, there will, perhaps, be several which have the heads of future bloom formed among the upper leaves. We have thus obtained young and blooming plants, which have expanded perfect flowers in April and May."

Although the above is rather a long quotation, yet as it is in strict accordance with a little-known but important principle of vegetable physiology, I have no hesitation in giving it to my readers. Nature in all her aspects is essentially reproductive, and under this general law all plants provide, either by seed or otherwise, for the increase and perpetuation of their species. Most plants, excepting Annuals, which I may term the spendthrifts of the vegetable kingdom, collect a greater store of nutriment, each season, than what is required for their consumption, just as the "busy bee" lays by honey for its support during winter, and the bleak flowerless days of early spring. Consequently if we take cuttings late in the season, we have this unexhausted store of nourishment in each cutting; besides, by giving roots to each, they will, as individuals, grow and flower better than if they were all—like a poor man's large family—depending for support upon the roots or exertions of the parent. On this principle cuttings of oleanders, hydrangeas, cacti, and many other plants, will flower sooner

and better if made late in the season. The only difficulty
is, that these late cuttings will require more care and trouble
to keep them alive during the winter than if they had been
made in the spring—but where there is no difficulty, there
is no honour.

KITCHEN GARDEN.

Cauliflowers, to stand through the winter under hand-
glasses, or in sheltered borders, and to come in for use in
spring, may be sown in the latter half of the month. Sow
in a bed of rich light mellow earth; water occasionally if the
weather is dry, until and after the plants appear above
ground. In September, when they have leaves an inch, or
an inch and a half broad, pick them out into an intermediate
bed three or four inches apart; water, and shade from the
mid-day sun until they have taken root. Those that you
intend to winter under hand-glasses must be finally
transplanted, in October, to a rich, well-manured spot of
ground. Place your hand-glasses in rows three feet asunder
each way. Put three or four plants under the centre of each
glass; give water, and cover close, until you observe that
the plants have struck root, which may be known by their
showing renewed growth; then admit air by tilting up the
south side of the glasses on fine days, but be careful to cover
close at night. Although the glasses must be kept over the
plants during the winter, yet it is essentially necessary to
take advantage of all temperate days by thus tilting up the
south side of the glasses. Indeed, in very fine mild days,
the plants will be all the better if totally uncovered until the
approach of evening. If the winter should prove excessively
inclement, it would be advisable to surround the glasses with
litter, or cover them with mats. Conforming thus to the
varying changes of the weather, you may continue to cover
with the glasses till May, giving more air as the genial
season of spring advances; and be sure, by uncovering, to

let the plants have the beneficial influence of any warm
gentle showers that may occur. In March, if the plants are
in good health—which they ought to be if the proper care, as
above described, has been taken of them—transplant into a
rich soil in the open ground, all excepting two, which you
may leave under each glass. Draw some earth up round the
stems of those left under the glasses, and as they advance in
growth, raise the glasses on props several inches high, for
the purposes of admitting air liberally and giving room for
the free growth of the plants. Continue to keep the glasses
over the plants as long as the latter have room to grow in
them. These plants under the glasses will be first fit for
use, then those planted out in March will follow in succession.

· If you do not possess glasses, you may, in October, prick
out the plants three inches apart, in a warm south border,
close under the wall, or fence ; protecting them in rigorous
weather with mats on hoops, dry litter, &c., giving air in
mild weather, and finally transplanting in March.

Mr. Ball finds, that if cauliflower seed is not sown till the
last week in August, and if the seedlings are not transplanted
till the middle or near the end of November, before the hard
weather sets in, no sort of covering is necessary, nor any
other protection than that of a wall having a south aspect :—
" In such a border, and without any covering, young cauliflower plants have stood well for many successive winters,
and have always proved better and sounder plants than such
as have had additional shelter. The seedlings protected
with glass generally grow too gross in the stems, which
become partly blackened ; and the plants being, thus
unhealthy, are not fit for planting out. Late-raised seedlings, which spend the winter in the open border, uniformly
become the largest and finest table cauliflowers during the
summer, though they certainly *do not come in quite so early.*
Cauliflower plants, it is probable, are often killed with too

much attention. Seedlings raised late in autumn seem to be very tenacious of life."—*Caledonian Horticultural Society's Mem.* iii. 192.

Dr. Johnson used to say:—"Of all the flowers in the garden, I like the cauliflower."

Dr. Neill (*Encyclopædia Edinensis*) observes, that the great quantities of cauliflowers fostered under glass during winter for the early supply of the London market—acres of ground being covered with such glasses—gives a stranger a forcible idea of the riches and luxury of the metropolis.

GARDENING FOR SEPTEMBER.

FLOWER GARDEN.

PERENNIAL and biennial flowering plants that have been raised from seed, layers, pipings, slips, or offsets, may now be finally transplanted to the beds or borders in which it is intended that they are to flower. Select those of the largest growth, transplant in rainy weather, and with a small ball of earth adhering to the roots of each plant : water carefully, and the plants will soon take root, and in the ensuing summer flower luxuriantly. Any fibrous-rooted plant that may have overspread into a large tuft should be reduced to a proper size by cutting off a portion—the part cut off may be planted where required. Almost all perennials may now be increased by dividing their roots ; the larger slips may be planted in the borders to flower next season, and the smaller put in nursery-beds to acquire strength and size. Fleshy-rooted plants, as Cyclamens, winter Aconites, Fraxinellas, Irises, and other similar-rooted plants, may now be safely taken up, their roots parted, and planted again ; they will be well established before winter, and consequently may be expected to produce strong flowers the ensuing summer.

F

Pansies may now be propagated, either by cuttings or by
division of their roots. The pansy is a florist's flower,
though but lately admitted into that brilliant class. A few
years ago it was little better than a weed; now, improved
by human art, it takes its place, with a graceful air of hu-
mility, among the proudest beauties of the floral kingdom.
The cuttings should be taken from the extremities of the
young shoots, and ought to be cut off just below the third
joint from the top, removing the leaves from the part that is
to be inserted in the soil. Plant them an inch or two apart
in a sheltered border, and in rather rich loamy soil that has
been been previously well watered. Cover with a hand-
glass, and if the sun shine strongly, shade with some light
material for a few days. In a short time the hand-glass may
be removed by degrees to admit light and air, and as soon
as the cuttings are well rooted they may be planted out
again in a similar situation. To have some in bloom early
next spring, a bed should be prepared now, and planted
with strong-rooted cuttings; these should be protected
through the winter in rigorous weather by a covering of
hoops and mats. Pansies in old beds should now be cut
down, and a little earth thrown up about them; this will
cause them to push up fresh roots, which may subsequently
be detached to form new plants. New varieties are obtained
from seed. The seed is taken from the first ripened pods of
the best sorts, and as soon as it is ripe sown thinly in a
shady situation, and light loamy soil. When the young
plants have formed a few leaves, they should be transplanted
to a similar bed, or border, at about four inches apart, and
after this they may be treated as the old plants. Pansies
always require a rich loamy soil, and a cool shady situation.
They are also considered to be great deteriorators of the soil,
consequently they should not be allowed to remain longer
than one year in the same place. For this reason, also,
gardeners never remove pansies as they do other plants,
with balls of earth adhering to their roots; on the contrary,

when transplanting pansies they carefully wash away all
the soil from the roots of each plant.

Window Gardening.

The *Tropæolum tricolorum*, the prettiest of window
climbers, may be planted this month; the tubers can be
obtained at any seed-shop. Plant each tuber—which is not
unlike a potato—eye upwards, and about an inch and a half
beneath the surface of a pot about nine inches in diameter,
well drained, and filled with a rich light soil. Give a little
water when you plant, and afterwards no more than will
just keep the soil in the pot moist until you find the plant
growing freely, then you may apply water as it seems to
require it. The shoots, as they advance, should be trained
to stakes, or a trellis, according to the taste or fancy of the
cultivator. A neat and tasteful method is to have a plant
on each side of the window, and train the shoots upward and
across until they meet at the top. The flowers, which
appear late in the spring, are exceedingly abundant and
beautiful, and, as the name implies, tricoloured—crimson,
orange, and black. After flowering, the plant dies completely down; the tubers should then be taken from the
pots, and kept in a dry place until the season for planting
again arrives.

Hardy bulbs planted in pots now, and kept in a warm airy
window, may be forced into flower very early next year.
The double Roman Narcissus, among others, has been highly
recommended for this purpose by Mr. Beaton, one of the
best practical gardening authorities of the day. They require a light soil, and three bulbs may be planted in a pot
of six inches in diameter. After planting give water, and
then set the pots in a shady place, "*where the heat of the
sun cannot reach to stimulate the bulbs to make leaves before
they have made roots*, for that (continues Mr. B.) is the
grand secret in forcing all kinds of bulbs." Several others
of the Narcissus tribe, the single and double Van Thol Tulip,

double and single Jonquils, and Hyacinths, are forced in
this way. Another most excellent mode of forcing these
bulbs, and on the very same principle, is to plunge the pots
containing them into the ground, and cover them to the
depth of six inches with old rotted bark, sawdust, or other
light material. As soon as the plants appear above the surface of the material used for covering, they should be removed to a window; there, if kept close to the light, and
well watered, they will flower in the greatest perfection.

KITCHEN GARDEN.

This month is the principal season for commencing one of
the most curious and singular operations in gardening—the
cultivation of Mushrooms. In every other gardening process
we sow or plant something tangible and material, be it seed,
slip, or root, but in this we plant merely "a white fibrous
substance, running like broken threads in such reduced
dung or other nidus as is fitted to nourish it." This substance is called mushroom spawn, and is found indigenous
in pastures, cattle sheds, covered rides for horses, dry, half
rotted dung-heaps, and various other situations. It is also
produced artificially by mixing different kinds of rotten
dung together. The indigenous spawn may, with care, be
preserved for two or three years by keeping it quite dry, and
in a constant current of air. The artificial spawn is preserved by being formed into what are termed bricks; in this
state, if kept dry, it can be preserved for many years, and
can be had from almost any nurseryman. I would advise
any of my readers who intend to try mushroom cultivation
for the first time, to use the brick-spawn; and after acquiring a little experience and knowledge to distinguish the
spawn, then, say next year, if they live in a locality where
indigenous spawn is obtainable, let them resort to the fields
for it. I can assure my readers, that by using the brick-
spawn, procured from a respectable nurseryman, many dis-
appointments will be avoided. Mushrooms are grown on

ridges in the open air, in sheds, cellars, &c. To form a
ridge, choose a dry spot of ground, and mark out your bed
four beds broad, and as long as you may require. Then,
with equal quantities of fresh and old dried stable-dung,
mixed well together, proceed to build the ridge, shaking and
mixing the dung, beating it well down with the fork, and
working it up in a sloping manner, so as to terminate
in a narrow roof-shaped ridge along the centre, about four
feet in height. The bed thus made should then be covered
with litter, and left to settle for a week or two, till the fiery
heat of the fermenting dung has passed away. When the
bed is cooled down to the proper temperature for receiving
the spawn, on a fine day remove the covering, and bank up
a couple of inches in depth of dry loamy earth all over the
ridge. Then dividing the spawn-bricks into moderately-
sized pieces, deposit each piece about six inches apart in the
earth banked up on the ridge; spread a thin stratum of
earth over all, beating it down firmly and smoothly with
the back of the spade. The ridge being now spawned, must
be covered with dry, clean straw, or litter, to protect it from
the weather. It must afterwards be frequently inspected, to
see if wet has penetrated to the spawn, and wherever this
has occurred, fresh dry spawn must be substituted. In
about six or seven weeks the ridge will begin to produce a
plentiful crop of mushrooms.

Mushrooms may also be grown in pots, boxes, hampers, or
other similar appliances, kept in dry, dark, frost-proof
cellars. By having several boxes, and preparing them at
different times in rotation, a supply of mushrooms for the
table may be had all the year round. Although the writer
has paid considerable attention to the fungi tribe of plants,
and conducted many experiments on the raising of mushrooms, yet he candidly confesses that he cannot recommend
a better plan than the following one, by Mr. Wales, abridged
from the Memoirs of the Caledonian Horticultural Society:
—"Each box may be three feet long, one and a-half broad,

and seven inches in depth. Let each box be half filled with
horse-dung from the stables (the fresher the better, and if
wet, to be dried for three or four days before it be put into
the boxes); the dung is to be well beat down in the box.
After the second or third day, if any heat has arisen amongst
the dung, break each spawn brick into three parts as equally
as possible, then lay the pieces about four inches apart upon
the surface of the dung in the box; here they are to lie for
six days, when it will probably be found that the side of the
spawn next to the dung has begun to run in the dung below;
then add one and a half inch more of fresh dung on the top
of the spawn in the box, and beat it down as formerly. In
the course of a fortnight, when you find that the spawn has
run through the dung, the box will be ready to receive the
mould on the top; this mould must be two and a half inches
deep, well beat down, and the surface made quite even. In
the space of five or six weeks the mushrooms will begin to
come up; if then the mould seems dry, give a gentle watering with lukewarm water. The box will continue to produce
from six weeks to two months, if duly attended to by giving
a little water when dry, for they need neither *light* nor *free
air*. If cut as button mushrooms, each box will yield from
twenty-four to forty-eight pints, according to the season and
other circumstances."

Mushrooms may also be grown in boxes, &c., without the
dung, and though by the latter method the produce is not
so large, yet their flavour is superior to those grown with
dung; indeed they cannot be distinguished from the natural
field mushroom. The mode is as follows:—

"Take a little straw, and lay it carefully in the bottom
of the mushroom-box, about an inch thick, or rather more.
Then take some of the spawn-bricks and break down
each brick into about ten pieces, and lay the fragments on
the straw, as close to each other as they will lie. Cover them
up with mould three and a half inches deep, and well pressed
down. When the surface appears dry, give a little tepid

water, as directed for the last way of raising them; but this method needs about double the quantity of water that the former does, owing to having no moisture in the bottom, while the other has the dung. The mushrooms will begin to start in a month or five weeks, sometimes sooner, sometimes later, according to the heat of the place where the boxes are situated."

During the first fortnight of the month, Lettuces may be sown, to stand over the winter, and come in for use early in the ensuing spring. Sow as directed in the *Gardening for March*, and when the plants are two or three inches high, a portion of them should be transplanted from the seed-bed to a warm piece of ground previously prepared for their reception. Here they are to remain through the winter, and for the convenience of covering they need not be more than six inches apart. Of those that you leave in the seed you may thin out a few for use in the winter, leaving some for spring. In severe weather they should be temporarily sheltered with mats on hoops, fern, reed hurdles, or similar contrivances; always, however, being careful to remove these coverings when the weather is mild.

Fruit.

In moist weather, during this month, will be a good time to plant Strawberries. Choose the largest offsets of the first spring runners, and plant in single rows along the edge of a walk, place the plants eighteen inches apart in the row, and if another row be made it should be two feet from the first one. Strawberries require a rich soil, deeply trenched, and well manured previous to planting: all runners and blossoms should be cut off the plants the first year, after that they will produce abundantly until the fourth year, when they should be dug up. For this season new rows of runners should be planted every year to keep up a succession. The Keen's Seedling, British Queen, Myatt's Pine, Elton Pine, and Black Prince, are of the best kinds. The Alpine strawberry is generally grown as an annual, from seed sown in a bed of rich soil early in the spring. In July or August, the young plants should be planted out in a moist soil, and in rows two feet asunder, the plants one foot apart in the row; they will produce fruit late in the same season, long after the other kinds of strawberries have done bearing.

———

GARDENING FOR OCTOBER.

FLOWER GARDEN.

PREPARATIONS should now be made for wintering the half hardy plants, which, after gladdening the borders in the summer months, require and deserve protection during the winter. Fuchsias (excepting the broad-leaved kinds, as *Fulgens corymbiflora*, &c., which should be kept in a window) go to rest naturally at this season of the year, and may be protected in the open ground by coverings of ashes, mats, sawdust,—anything, in short, that will preserve their roots from frost. But as the stems and branches will, in all probability, be killed, the plants of next year will be merely a cluster of suckers sent up by the root. So all standard or other fuchsias, the stems and branches of which you wish to preserve, should be taken up, the soil shaken from their roots, the plants laid together in a dry frost-proof outhouse or cellar, and their roots covered with dry sand until the beginning of April, when you may plant them out again. Fuchsias, trained to walls, may be preserved by their roots being well covered with ashes, and their stems and branches by mats nailed to the wall. If this plan is inconvenient, the plant may be taken up, and the laterals or side-shoots trimmed off as you would a walking-stick, leaving from three to six stems, about five or six feet long. Having prepared a pit, in dry soil or sand, three feet deep and as long as required, bury your fuchsias with a little straw about them, and fill up the pit, leaving the surface in a sharp ridge so as to throw off the water. About the end of April dig them up; you will find them growing vigorously: plant and train to the wall as before.

Scarlet Geraniums only require to be kept cool, just free from frost, and dry. About ten days before taking up the plants, all the large leaves, and any young watery shoots apparently too soft to last the winter, should be carefully cut off. When the plants are taken up, every leaf should be stripped off; and the plants may be hung up by the roots in a dry, dark cellar, or covered with dry hay, and put away in a box in any garret, lumber-room, or hayloft, that is cool, dry, and frost-proof. A plan of wintering these plants, when grown in large pots and boxes, recommended by the best authority, and which I have proved, is to cut off every leaf before the plants are touched by frost, and to keep them all winter in a dry, cool room, without giving one drop of water. In March put them out on fine sunny days, bringing them in at night, still keeping them dry till the young leaves appear, when you may commence to give water. By this method the plants do not require re-potting for several years. Not only the whole plant, but cuttings of this semi-succulent kind of geranium may be kept dry all winter. Take cuttings now from six inches to a foot in length, keep them in a cool, airy room, for about a month, till they are quite dry; then wrap them up separately in paper, or put them away in a drawer or dry cupboard. About midwinter examine them, and if any black spots, or gangrenous decay, appear at the end of the cuttings, cut it out. In March you may pot them, give water, and keep in a warm room; they will soon form roots, and be ready for turning out into the open ground by May.

Scarlet (*Mexican*) Salvias should be cut down before frost, and the roots, with the soil adhering to them, lifted, and kept during winter in dry sand, in any place free from damp

and frost; in April the roots will begin to grow, and then
they may be divided and planted out again. The blue salvia
(*Salvia patens*) having roots containing eyes, similar to those
of the dahlia, may be treated in the same manner as that
plant; lift the roots, keep them dry, and plant; cut in spring.

Calceolarias, Verbenas, and their cuttings, require to be
wintered in a light, airy window, and kept perfectly
free from damp—next to frost their deadliest winter
enemy.

The bloom of many plants may be prolonged to very late
in the season, by giving timely shelter from the first autumnal frosts. Geraniums, Dahlias, Helitropes, Chrysanthemums,
&c., may be sheltered by mats during frosty nights; and as
it frequently occurs that after the first few frosty nights we
have no more for a month or two, so by sheltering these
plants from the first frost, we can preserve them in bloom
for a considerable time longer.

Walks may now be made, and edgings laid down. The
dwarf Dutch Box affords the neatest edging, and if annually
clipped lasts in good order for many years. The Thrift
forms a very pretty edging, but it has to be renewed every
few years. The Double Daisy, Stemless Gentian (*Gentiana
acaulis*), London Pride, and Saxifraga hypnoides—all these
make beautiful edgings. Other plants suitable for edgings,
but not so commonly used for that purpose, are the Pansy,
Dwarf Bellflower (*Campanula pumila*), Cowslip, Polyanthus,
Auricula, Hepatica, *Veronica fructiculosa, Culluna vulgaris,
Flore plesso,* and *Erica carnea.* Neat edgings may also be
formed by narrow stripes, or as they are termed, verges of
grass turf.

Take care of such flowers as still retain their beauty, pick
off all dead buds and leaves, and draw earth up to their
stems. Keep the walks clear of weeds, and remove all
decayed stems, leaves, flowers, flower-stakes, and litter of
any kind out of the garden; so that a sober neatness may
succeed the summer's gaiety.

Evergreen Shrubs.

Now is about the best season of the whole year for transplanting evergreen shrubs. Have them taken up with as large a ball of earth adhering to their roots as possible. Dig the hole to receive the shrub larger than the size of the ball, but not so deep as to place the roots of the shrub lower in the soil than they were before. Loosen the earth at the bottom of the hole, and pour in water to form a puddle; put in the shrub, carefully spreading and laying out flat any straggling roots or root-fibres. Then throw in a few inches in depth of earth over the roots, and pour in more water to settle the earth about them, proceeding so until the hole be filled. The shrub may then be tied to stakes, to keep it steady in high winds; and a layer of litter placed round the stem, as far as the roots diverge, will ensure success to the operation. Cuttings of Laurels, Phillyreas, Jasmine, Aucuba, Holly, Box, Honeysuckle, and other evergreen and deciduous shrubs may now be taken and planted. Choose strong shoots of last summer's growth, from nine to eighteen inches in length; strip off all the lower leaves, leaving but a few at the top, and plant the cuttings half their length deep in the soil of a shady border, pressing the earth with your foot firmly about them. They will soon root, and be fit for transplanting in about twelve months.

Window Gardening.

All tender plants, young cuttings, &c., that must be kept in a growing state during the winter, should be placed inside the window immediately, (*September 15th*,) as an hour's frost would be fatal, and the weather at this time of the year is very uncertain.

The *Camellia Japonica*, though introduced into this country from China, is, as the name implies, a native of Japan, and of the same genus as the Camellias, *Bohea* and *Viridis*, which supply the well-known black and green teas of commerce.

It is truly a superb plant, combining the rich blossoms of the rose with the glossy foliage of the evergreen; and though sufficiently hardy to live and produce a few insignificant weather-beaten flowers out of doors in this climate, yet, from some peculiarities in its constitution and in the formation of its flower-buds, the camellia requires great care and attention before it deigns to expand its gorgeous petals even in a window. The principal difficulty is, that the flower-buds, when formed, are exceedingly liable to drop off from the plant previous to their expansion. This unfortunate habit, when it occurs, is attributed to a too great or a too small supply of water, and also to a too great variation of temperature, particularly when the buds are swelling. To flower the camellia in perfection, a higher temperature than that of a greenhouse is requisite during what is termed the growing season. Still, with care, it can be flowered beautifully in a window, without any artificial heat whatever, more than the average temperature of a sitting-room. The routine of window-cultivation commences when the plant has done flowering, at which time, if it is a young, small-sized plant, it should be shifted into a pot of a size larger, but if an old large plant, it need not be re-potted oftener than once in two years. The soil should be composed of equal parts of peat and loam ; and, as peat cannot be procured in every locality, the next best soil is light, sandy loam, enriched with a small quantity of leaf-mould. After potting, the plant should be placed in the window of a rather close, warm room, where a fire is kept; and there it is to remain as long as it continues growing, and until the flower-buds for the ensuing season are perfectly developed. During this time, when the plant is growing and the flower-buds forming, water should be rather liberally supplied ; the leaves and branches should also be frequently sprinkled with water; and the dust which, even in the tidiest room, *will* adhere to the leaves, carefully washed off with a sponge. The plant should have as much light as possible, but extreme care should be taken, in all stages of the camellia's growth, never to let the sun's rays shine directly upon it. When the plant has ceased growing, it should then be put out of doors in a shaded situation, where, at most, it will be exposed to the early morning's sun only, and where it will be sheltered from cold winds. There it is to be kept till about this season of the year, or rather earlier—for it must on no account have the slightest acquaintance with frost—when it should again be placed in the window. The plant, if in good health, and if the preceding directions have been adhered to, will be well furnished with flower-buds; and now is the critical season, when all care is required to prevent these buds from falling off before they expand into beauteous flowers. Water must be carefully applied, the soil in the pot must never be permitted to become dry, nor yet should it be always soaking wet. Observe that at this time, either one hour's drought, or the soil in the pots becoming soddened, will equally bring down the buds, thereby destroying your hopes, and rendering nugatory all your previous care. The temperature of the room should not be higher than fifty, nor lower than thirty-five degrees. A medium temperature between the two suits the camellia best at this stage of its culture. The room should not be too close; neither should the plant stand in a draught. If it is inconvenient to open the window, and the out-door temperature not less than forty degrees, the plant may be placed outside for a couple of hours in the middle of the day; but be extremely careful that it be not where the sun can shine upon it. As the buds swell for flowering, a little more water may be given; do not give water little and often, but give a good dose at once, and then wait until the plant requires it again; with a well-drained pot no injury, but much benefit, will accrue from this mode of watering the camellia. Never let a drop of water remain in the saucer beneath the pot. After your camellia has flowered—as, gentle reader, I sincerely hope it will—the same routine of culture must be gone through again.

There are a great many varieties of the camellia, and its

popularity is almost universal; the Italians, Germans, and Americans vieing with John Bull in the production of new and beautiful varieties. To the window gardener who has room for only one or two plants, I would recommend the double white and double red kinds. The camellia is propagated by seeds, cuttings, grafting, and in-arching; but as these processes are difficult, and can only be properly performed by practical gardeners, I consider that I need not further allude to them.

KITCHEN GARDEN.

Carrots and Beet should now be stored away for winter use. The best mode of keeping these roots is to place them in alternate layers of dry sand, either in the corner of a dry cellar, or in barrels or boxes. A layer of sand an inch thick should be first laid down, and upon it a layer of the roots, then another inch in depth of sand between each alternate layer of roots, until all are stored away, when the heap should be covered with about four inches of sand. Some cut off the extreme top or bud at the thick end of the carrot, to prevent it from growing; but I have never found this precaution necessary. Though rather out of place here, I may observe that if the top of a carrot cut off at this season, or later, is placed in a shallow vessel with water, it will grow, forming a radiated feathery tuft of very handsome appearance, and by no means unworthy of being placed on any drawing-room mantelpiece, as a beautiful and interesting ornament.

Parsnips may be stored in the same manner as carrots; but as the former not only can endure, but even are improved by the hardest frost, they need not be taken up, except a few for use at any time that the ground may be frozen too hard.

Onions keep best when made up into ropes, and the ropes kept in a cool, dry place.

The Chive (*Allium schœnoprasum*)—commonly termed by

the plural, chives, or lyse, from a quantity being taken for
use at one time—is, though a native plant, seldom seen in
English gardens, but well known and common in Scotland,
where it is much used for seasoning broths, soups, omelets,
salads, and other culinary preparations. As it has a mild
and agreeable flavour, and takes up very little room, no
garden should be without it. It is propagated by slips,
or by dividing the roots in spring or autumn. Any one who
can procure a few roots now, should plant them about six
inches apart; they will soon increase into patches. When
gathering the leaves for use, cut close to the ground; others
will soon shoot up in their places. After the bed has lasted
for three or four years, it should be renewed by separating
the roots, and planting them in a fresh place.

The fallen tree-leaves, wherever practicable, should be
carefully collected. As leaf-mould should form a part of the
soil of almost all potted plants, it is peculiarly valuable to
the window gardener. The leaves, when collected for this
purpose, should be laid in a flat heap exposed to the rain,
and turned frequently to expedite their decomposition.
When thoroughly rotted, so as to crumble into powder when
rubbed between the thumb and finger, the leaf-mould is fit
for use. Leaves are also used for supplying, by their fer-
mentation, artificial heat in hotbeds. For this purpose the
leaves should be made up in a ridge-shaped pile, to keep
them from getting too wet, turned over, and well mixed
every three weeks. If quite dry, a little water should be
thrown on the heap as it is turned over, and fresh-gathered
leaves added and mixed with the others. In spring the
leaves will be in condition to make a hotbed of moderate,
but lasting heat. Leaves also may be gathered in a heap,
house-slops thrown on them, road-scrapings added if pro-
curable, and in spring dug into the ground as manure.

All vacant ground should now be trenched, and thrown
up into ridges, to receive the ameliorating effects of winter's
frosts.

GARDENING FOR NOVEMBER.

FLOWER GARDEN.

THE flower beds and borders should—if not previously done —be now carefully dug over, all decayed stems removed, manure dug in if the soil is too poor, and the surface raked neat and smooth, as you must commence immediately to plant your bulbs, and until they appear above ground in spring, you cannot well dig over the borders without disturbing and destroying many of the favourite plants. Tulip and Hyacinth bulbs should be planted early in the month. If planted in beds, they should be placed in rows nine inches asunder, and not less than six inches between each plant—the bulbs three inches deep, beneath the surface of the soil. If planted in the borders, they may be placed in a continued row, about eighteen inches from the walk, or in small patches of three, four, or five bulbs together. Be careful to plant tulips and hyacinths in such beds or borders as are driest throughout the winter, as these bulbs are liable to receive damage, and even to rot, if the ground is too wet. Crocuses and Snowdrops should also now be planted, either in small patches, or in continued rows round the borders, about nine inches from the edge or walk. Narcissuses, Jonquils, Crown Imperials, Fritillarias, Martagons, bulbous Iris, Star of Bethlehem, Grape Hyacinths, Lilies, Aconites, should now be planted. Choose a dry open day for the purpose. They may be placed in small patches of from three to four, five, or six in each patch, according to their size; and always be careful to put the tallest growing plants in the middle of the bed, or at the back of the border. Anemones and Ranunculuses may be planted now, though the choicer sorts should not be put into the ground before February—see *Gardening* for that month. Roses may be transplanted during the winter months, and propagated by removing their suckers; and wild-rose stocks, for budding

upon next season, may now be transplanted from the fields
and hedges to any out-of-the-way part of the garden.

Window Gardening.

I have given some directions for the winter treatment of
some particular window plants : in my former papers I have
always mentioned the winter treatment of each plant whose
culture I described. Upon consideration, the best general
directions that I can now give for wintering such plants as
I have not previously alluded to, are :—That those plants
which naturally go to rest in winter should be kept dry, in
a rather cool room just free from frost; and those which
continue in a growing state should be kept in a warmer
room, and occasionally watered. In severe weather, when
the fire is extinguished at night, the plants should be taken
down from the window, and put below a table; and if the
weather is rigorously frosty, they may be covered, when in
that situation, with a sheet. Those persons who grow Hyacinths in water-glasses should now plant the bulbs in pots,
with loose, sandy soil, and keep them in a dark place until
they make roots three inches in length. The soil should
then be washed away from the bulbs, and root-fibres carefully introduced into the glasses, which should be filled with
soft, tepid water, just so high as not to touch the lower part
of the bulb. The water ought to be renewed every four or
five days with fresh tepid water. Hyacinths, and several
other bulbs, may also be grown in pots filled with fresh
damp moss : the bulbs are not so much weakened by this
method as they are when flowered in water.

Bunyan, in his amusing and instructive allegory, the
"Pilgrim's Progress," after conducting "Christian" through
the perils of the "dark valley," leads him past the caves of
the two noted giants who had formerly perpetrated a deal
of mischief, but were too old and feeble to injure man-
kind. A similar giant, once very mischievous, now by the
improved usages of society rendered almost harmless, may

G

be found laid on the shelf in many a corner-cupboard and china-closet. It would be well to make the old-fashioned tyrannical deceiver useful now, by way of atonement for its former sins. The ancient Greeks crowned their Bacchanalian cups and vases with flowers. The ancient Egyptians placed a skeleton as a *memento mori* at their festive boards. Let us, with purer motives, do the same. Wherever there is a china punch-bowl, let it be filled with flowers, and placed on the table, as the warning skeleton of past folly, and as a trophy of the great victory gained by innocent refinement over sottish and sensual debauchery. Hyacinths, Tulips, Narcissuses, Crocuses, and Snowdrops, may all be grown in light soil or damp moss, in pots or other utensils; and when kept in a room during winter, not too warm at first, they will come into flower earlier than if they were grown in the open air. I can assure the reader that a punch-bowl filled with any of these plants in a growing state, whether they be in flower or not, is a very handsome ornament, fit for any apartment. The bulbs may be disposed according to the taste of the planter, but the tallest growing should be placed in the centre of the bowl. If the plants are all of the same kind and size, the centre of the soil or moss should be higher than at the sides, so as to present a slightly convex surface. Crocuses may be planted as thickly as you can place them, and covered about an inch in depth. If purple, yellow, white, and lilac crocuses are planted in concentric circles, each of one colour, round the bowl, they will have a pleasing effect when in flower. Tulips should be planted at the same depth as crocuses; the hyacinth bulbs just barely covered. The double Roman narcissus grows well in moss, and forms a fine centre-plant for the floral bowl.

KITCHEN GARDEN.

The delicious vegetable, Sea-Kale (*Crambe maritima*), though indigenous to the gravelly shores of England, was not cultivated as a garden esculent until the latter part of the last century. It thrives best in a light, dry soil, manured with half-rotten tree leaves, or, where it can be procured, sea-weed. The ground should be prepared in December, by trenching two feet and a half deep; if the soil is too heavy, it should be lightened by mixing with it sand, road scrapings, or ashes; and if too poor, it should be enriched by some old rotten manure. In March lay out the ground into beds four feet wide, then mark out stations in the beds two feet apart each way, and at each station sow five or six seeds, two inches deep, in a circle of four inches in diameter. When the young plants have made three or four leaves, take away all but three out of each circle; and if the summer proves dry give plenty of water. In November, or as soon as the leaves decay, pick them off, and cover the beds an inch thick with light, sandy soil; and over that lay about six inches in depth of light stable-litter. In the next spring rake off the litter, and add another inch of light soil. Abstain from cutting this second year, treating the beds in winter as before. The third spring, when the plants begin to grow, rake off the winter covering of litter, and lay on an inch in depth of pure sand or ashes. Then cover each cluster of plants with a blanching-pot, pressing it firmly into the ground, so as to exclude both light and air. When the young shoots are fit for use, they should be cut off carefully, without injuring the remaining buds, some of which will immediately swell and grow, affording a succession of gatherings for about six weeks; then the plants should be uncovered and their leaves suffered to grow, that they may acquire and supply nutriment to the roots, so as to enabl the latter to produce next year's buds. The flowers should be carefully picked off as long as they continue to appear. To give the reader an idea of the extent of ground he may require-for sea-kale, I may say that one blanching pot covering three plants should furnish two good dishes each season. Half butter-barrels, which may be procured at the butter-shops, though not so convenient, are good substitutes for blanching-pots, and are not so expensive. The cleanest, neatest, and best mode of blanching sea-kale is by the use of these pots. Some, however, do not use them, but cover the beds in autumn with tree-leaves, from five inches to a foot in depth, laying a little long litter on the top, to prevent the leaves from being blown about. As the shoots become fit for use they protrude through the covering, and can be readily cut by removing a few of the adjacent leaves. The beds which are thickest covered come into bearing first, so by attending to this, a succession may be kept up.

The reverend and talented gentleman who has written so many practically useful works under the *nom de plume* of "Martin Doyle," gives the following process by which sea-kale sown in March may be cut the following Christmas:—
" Trench the ground to the depth of eighteen inches, and dig in a compost of coal-ashes strongly impregnated with night-soil, or if this cannot be procured, with any rich compost. When the soil is perfectly dry and friable, form the beds of the size most convenient, with a fall from the centre. Early in March, should the weather be favourable, draw the drills with the hoe, at intervals of eighteen inches by two and a half or three inches deep; drop the seeds four inches apart, and fill in the drills by drawing the mould gently back with a rake. Keep the plants free from weeds, and in the progress of their growth be careful not to allow the soil to become encrusted about them by heavy rains and a hot sun, but keep the earth loose, by carefully stirring it so as to promote the expansion of the fibres without injuring the plant. When the leaves begin to decay—perhaps early in September—cut them off, and cover the drills with dry screened coal-ashes, to the height of eighteen inches. In the beginning of November cover the whole surface of the bed, both drills and intervals, with fresh good stable-litter to the height of two and a half feet. By this culture the plants will be as much matured against Christmas and the first week of January as those of three years' standing

would be in the ordinary way. Should February be mild and open, the seed may be sown and the process advanced one month earlier."

No vegetable is so cheaply and easily forced as sea-kale. About three weeks before you wish to cut the shoots put on the blanching-pots, and lay some warm dung or fermenting leaves—a mixture of both is best—over and round the pots, to the depth of about eight inches. Examine the plants frequently, and find by a thermometer the degree of heat inside the pot; for if it be above 60 deg., it is too fiery, and may injure the plants; and if below 50 deg., not warm enough to excite them to rapid action. In about three weeks the first shoots will be fit to cut; if the plant send up a flower-stalk, cut it away. Successive supplies of shoots may be obtained for nearly three months from the commencement of forcing. Sea-kale may also be forced and blanched in any dark warm cellar, or cupboard. Take up the plants as soon as their leaves are decayed, and pack them thickly in a box, filling up with light soil. Three successive cuttings may thus be obtained. In April the roots may be planted out in the garden again, and by plentiful waterings with liquid manure, brought round so as to be fit for forcing again the same winter. However, as the plants must be considerably weakened by this treatment, the best plan is to raise from seed every year, and force in this manner the plants of two seasons' growth.

Parsley.—If a few strong roots of this useful herb be taken up now, and planted in pots or boxes, and these taken in-doors, or kept in shelter, they will afford a supply for the table during any severe frosts that may very probably occur through the winter.

Fruit.

Gooseberries may be planted during open weather any time from now till March. Bushes, procured from a nursery, about three years old, with pretty full heads, are the best

for immediate, fruitful bearers. They like a loose, rich soil,
which readily imbibes but does not retain much moisture.
The gooseberry may be propagated by all the methods applicable to trees or shrubs; but cuttings are most usually taken
to continue and multiply known kinds, and seed sown when
the object is to obtain new varieties. The best time to plant
cuttings is during this and the previous month. They should
be about a foot long, and taken from the bearing shoots of a
medium size. Cut off the top, and all the buds except the
four uppermost; it is said that the cuttings strike root better
if they are slipped off, and if two or three shallow notches
are made in the bark, at the lower end of each, to facilitate
the sprouting of root fibres. They may be planted at first
only a few inches apart, until they are well rooted, when
they should be transplanted into a rich nursery bed, in rows
two feet apart, and one foot between each plant in the row.
All suckers and shoots on the lower part of the stem must
be cut off, leaving only four shoots at the top, and these cut
back to about six inches in length. In the second year they
may be planted out where they are to remain. If in a com-
partment by themselves, the bushes should now be in rows
six feet apart, and four feet from bush to bush. In a small
garden, however, they should be planted round the edges of
the compartments, about three feet from the path. The
ground will then be clear for cropping, and a person by
setting one foot on the border can gather the fruit without
injuring anything else. This second season two shoots ought
to be allowed to grow on each of the four leading ones, and
all others cut away, leaving those eight shoots to form a
head. The ensuing year the bushes will come into bearing.
There are many different modes of training the gooseberry
bush; one very suitable for a small garden is to train it to
a single stem, with spurs only, and no branches. The stem
is tied to a stake. This, though six or eight feet high,
occasions scarcely any shade on the border, takes up less
room than any other mode of training, nor does it exclude

air from other crops; while at the same time the stem, close hung with fruit, makes rather an ornamental appearance. The best general directions for training are, that if the fruit is intended to be gathered when green, the thicker the bush, and the more numerous the shoots, the better; but when it is intended that the fruit should ripen, the centre of the bush should always be kept open, so as freely to admit light and air. Gooseberries require but little summer pruning—merely the cross and watery shoots which crowd the heart of the bush should be cut out. For their winter pruning see *Gardening for January*. The ground about the bushes should be dug once a year, and manure, if required, dug in at the same time. No further culture is requisite than to keep free from weeds, and prevent the ravages of caterpillars, which frequently do serious injury; the best defence against them is carefully picking them off by hand.

Red and White Currants may now be planted; they are propagated by cuttings in a similar manner as gooseberries. They will do well in any kind of common garden soil, but thrive best in warm, moist, airy situations. They are generally trained as bushes, from single stems about a foot in height. When pruning, cut out all cross and irregular branches, and such as are old and barren; retain the best placed shoots for succession, cutting them back to about six inches in length; superfluous side shoots should be cut down to short stubs about half an inch long, so that they may produce fruit-shoots and spurs.

Black Currants may now be planted. They thrive best in a moist deep soil, and shady situation, and are propagated and pruned as gooseberries; though in the latter operation you must depend less upon spurs, and more on the previous year's wood, for producing fruit.

Raspberries may now be planted. Although the root or stool of the raspberry is perennial, the stems or canes are only biennial. The fruit is produced on small branches, which grow from the stems of the previous year. Every year the stools throw up a number of canes, which bear fruit the subsequent season and then die. The raspberry is propagated by these canes or suckers of one season's growth, which should be taken from healthy, vigorous plants, in full bearing. Where raspberries are cultivated extensively, it is best to keep them by themselves, in rows from four to six feet asunder, according to the size of the plants, and from three to four feet apart in the row. They grow well in any good garden soil, but it is all the better if a little moist. Keep the young plants free from weeds during summer, and frequently loosen the soil about them. If the plants are strong they will produce a small quantity of fruit the first summer, as well as young canes for bearing in greater plenty the following year. As they get established, let all straggling suckers be taken off to admit the sun and air to the fruit. In November cut out all the old dead stems close to the ground, and having selected from the strongest young shoots on each main stool, three, four, or five, to be preserved for bearers, cut away all the rest. The shoots retained should have their tops cut off just below the weak, bending part, leaving them, in the smaller plants, three or four, and in the larger kinds, five or six feet in length. As the canes are too weak to stand alone, they should be tied together at the top, so as to antagonise and mutually support each other. After pruning dig the ground between and about the plants. A little rich manure dug in each winter would be highly beneficial. Fresh plantations of raspberries should be made every six or seven years.

GARDENING FOR DECEMBER.

FLOWER GARDEN.

ALL half-hardy plants, as Hydrangeas, Fuchsias, &c., left in the open borders out of doors, should have their roots protected by long dung, ashes, fern, or similar substances. Hardy plants in pots, that are intended to be kept out of doors, should be plunged in the ground during the winter; and some coal-ashes laid beneath them, to prevent worms entering the pots. If there is no room to plunge the pots, surround them with sand, ashes, straw, &c., as the frost is very apt to take effect on such plants when unprotected. Now is a good time for transplanting and moving all kinds of flowering shrubs. A very beautiful and interesting class of plants is the climbing flowering shrubs, and yet how many bare, unsightly walls we every day see that might be clad in mantles of rich verdure. The *Vistaria sinensis* is one of the most beautiful of this description of plants. The *Ceanothus azureus* (the blue red-wood) is also very ornamental. Though these two plants are rather tender, yet on a south wall, not much exposed to bleak winds, they will flower well, even in the northern parts of the kingdom. The evergreen thorn (*Cratægus pyracantha*) is grown chiefly for the beauty of the gorgeous clusters of red berries which it produces at this season of the year, when all else is barren gloom. The Virginia Creeper, (*Ampelopsis hederacea*,) is also much admired for the rich red tints which its leaves assume in the autumn months. The *Zecoma radicans* is well adapted for training up the front of a house; its rich orange and scarlet trumpet-shaped flowers being exceedingly abundant. The different varieties of Clematis, the hardy varieties of the Passion-flower (*Passiflora cerulea*), Honeysuckle, Jasmine, &c., are well known. The common ivy itself affords a rich green screen, pleasing to the eye, though it be enveloped in snow-flakes. Some climbing shrubs, as the Westaria, produce long straight shoots; these may be trained in a regular manner; others, as the Jasmine, throw out irregular lateral or side shoots, so that it is impossible to train them in order without depriving them of the branches which would produce flowers in the ensuing season. The different varieties of Jasmine and Clematis may be freely pruned in winter, but they should not be deprived of their laterals in summer, as it is from the extremities of these that the flowers are produced; instead, then, of cutting them off, the principal shoots should be fastened to the wall, and the shorter ones allowed to protrude from it. When the shrubs have grown so as to cover the wall, the best plan is to prune the young laterals to short spurs in the winter; such spurs will produce more lateral shoots in the succeeding summer, and from each of the latter's points will grow a cluster of flowers. If this system of spurring the young shoots in the winter, and allowing them free liberty in the summer, is carefully attended to, an exuberant display of flowers will be produced. The Passion-flower produces its curious flower on the wood of the same year's growth; so, in pruning, it should be cut back close to the old wood; besides, the shoots break better from the old wood than even that of two years' standing. An elegant way of growing climbing plants is to train them up a pole: few, that have not seen a westaria in flower, trained in this manner, can conceive the fine effect produced. The beauties—the glories of a pillar rose, are beyond description, though I hope that the manner of training and treating such plants is not. Honeysuckles, *Corchorus Japonica*, and various kinds of roses, and Virgin's-bower (*Clematis florida*), are admirably adapted for training up the stems of trees. The general complaint I hear, among brother amateurs, is, "I have no room." What! no room, with that red brick wall, or unsightly tarred fence, staring you in the face? Come, come, my friends, cover your walls, put up poles for climbing plants. You will have more show, more flowers, and add greatly to what the French term the *tout ensemble* of your garden! Low-growing flowering shrubs may be pruned at this season. In doing so, all the long straggling shoots of the last summer's growth which extend considerably beyond the other branches should either be cut close down, or trimmed regular with their neighbour. Any low, straggling growth, and all dead wood should be cut out. It is difficult to give any general rule for such operations, but the great object is to keep the shrubs distinct and clear from each other, so that every different plant may be plainly seen. However, where certain shrubs are planted in beds to form a mass, or as a shade, shelter, or blind for some unsightly object, no more pruning is required than merely to shorten the long, out-growing, rambling branches. After the shrubs are pruned, the ground between them should be dug over, and all suckers rising from the roots taken away.

Any composts that have been prepared for the flower-garden should be frequently turned over, so as thoroughly to receive the mellowing and insect-killing influence of frost. In mild, open weather, you may dig and prepare the beds and borders ready for planting flower roots in the spring.

Window Gardening.

Little can be added to my previous instructions respecting the winter management of this class of plants. Frost and damp must be excluded; air and light freely admitted. Plants in a lively growing state should be occasionally watered, all others kept perfectly dry. Until now, I have not had space to speak of a most interesting contrivance, which all who are lovers of the vegetable kingdom should endeavour to procure. Some years ago, a gentleman, living almost in the centre of London, invented an appliance for growing plants in rooms, and by which he successfully cultivated ferns and other sensitive plants, to whose consti-

tution the fuliginous atmosphere of large towns is certain
death. Mr. Ward, the gentleman alluded to, with great
praiseworthy liberality communicated his discovery to the
public, and Wardian cases for growing plants became very
fashionable for some time. But, in most instances, they
were *only* fashionable. Mrs. Brown got a Wardian case
because she saw one at the Joneses, and Mrs. Robinson got
one because Mrs. Brown had; this is proved by the very
few we now see. True lovers of Nature, who procured these
cases, kept them; but those who purchased them for mere
display soon got tired of the *"stupid things,"* as I have
more than once had the inestimable honour of hearing them
called. Now, the reason I am mentioning this is to let my
readers know, that, in consequence of this change of fashion,
Wardian cases may now be found for sale in brokers' shops
at half their original prices, though any person handy with
tools might make one for himself—indeed, the best. one I
ever saw was made by a labourer; and as I hope to be in
his part of the country at Christmas, I shall endeavour to
see him, and procure full instructions for making a similar
one, for the benefit of any reader who may require them.

A Wardian case is simply an oblong box, about five
inches in depth, with a ledge round about its rim. On this
ledge rests a glazed frame, about as high as it is long, the
whole forming a miniature spanroofed conservatory. The
top, or glazed frame, is not fastened to the box, more than
fitting close to the grooved ledge so that it can be lifted off
when requisite, to clean the glass, remove or put in the
plants, &c. A small window in the centre of the frame is
an acquisition ; for when the exterior atmosphere is of a
lower temperature than that within the case, the moisture,
condensing, attaches itself to the glass—just as we often see
it on the windows of our sitting-rooms in winter—and ob-
scures the plants from view. Now, when that occurs, if the
window be opened for a short time, the moisture will
evaporate, and the tiny garden again become visible. War-

dian cases are peculiarly applicable for growing that beautiful
and interesting tribe of plants—the Ferns, and also the
equally interesting, but much more difficult to cultivate,
British Orchids. In fact, it is almost impossible to grow
ferns or English orchids in towns without using the Wardian
case. The case should, in all circumstances, be perfectly
free from frost; if it is placed in a balcony or window-
sill, hardy plants should only be grown in it; but if it is
kept in a room where there is a fire, exotic plants will do
well in it. The soil, if ferns or orchids are grown, must be
a rough fibrous peat, broken by hand into small pieces; as
much peat as would be required for a case could, in towns,
be easily and cheaply procured from any nurseryman or
florist. The plants in these cases require very little water;
however, care should be taken to give some when the soil
appears dry; and it is best to apply it in a tepid state, in the
morning, leaving the window of the case open for an hour
or two, for the purpose of carrying off the superfluous at-
mospheric moisture.

A gentleman of great experience has favoured me with the
following list of ferns suitable for cultivation in a Wardian
case kept in a room where there is a fire in winter:—*Asplenium obtusatum* (obtuse spleenwort), *Lycopodium stolo-
niferum* (creeping club-moss), *Aspidium proliferum* (pro-
liferous shield-fern), *Adiantum cuneatum* (wedge-leaved
maiden's-hair), *Asplenium odontitis* (tooth-leaved spleenwort), *Doodia aspera* (rough doodia). These six ferns, or
others, will be sufficient for a small case, with other plants.
A great error, frequently committed, is crowding the case
too much. Other curious plants that will grow in a case
are:—*Saracenia purpurea* (purple side-saddle flower), *Saracenia flava* (yellow ditto), *Cypripedium insignum* (noble lady's
slipper), *Cypripedium venustum* (charming ditto), *Yucca
pilamentosa variegata* (variegated thready Adam's needle),
and several of the woody mesembryanthemums, commonly
called ice-plants. The following plants may also be sus-

pended from the roof of this miniature hothouse: *Epiphyllum truncatum*, *E. truncatum violaceum*, *Cereus flagelliformis* (vulgarly termed the rat-tailed cactus), *Tillandsia purpurea*, *Linaria cymbalaria variegata*. Some of the longer-leaved ferns, also, thrive well when thus suspended. The plants for this purpose should be taken out of their pots, and their balls of earth surrounded with moss, and bound round with copper wire, a loop being twisted on the end of the wire, to hang up the plant by, to a small hook inserted in the top of the case. I am informed, though I have not seen any, that little pots of that ubiquitous substance, gutta percha, are manufactured and used for the same purpose.

KITCHEN GARDEN.

Asparagus (*Asparagus officinalis*) is a hardy perennial plant, a native of Britain, though, in its wild state, rare; it is principally found in stony, gravelly soils, by the sea shore. The steppes of the east of Europe, in the southern parts of Russia and Poland, are covered with this plant, which is there eaten by the horses and oxen as grass. In its uncultivated state, it is so dwarfish in appearance, even when in flower, that no one but an experienced botanist would detect it to be the same species as our garden plant. The use of asparagus, as an esculent, is of considerable antiquity; it was a choice favourite with the Romans, who seem to have possessed a very strong growing variety; for Pliny mentions that three shoots would weigh a pound; with us it requires about six of the largest to turn the scale at that weight.

Asparagus, growing naturally in loose sand, should have a light, deep soil, through which it may be able to shoot its long stringy roots. The ground should be trenched to the depth of two feet and a half, and a considerable portion of old rotted manure, or recently-gathered sea weed, laid in the bottom of the trench. The general custom of growing asparagus is in beds four or five feet wide, with intervening alleys of about eighteen inches in breadth. Within the last few years, however, a method has come into general practice of growing in rows from three to four feet apart. This latter plan is said to be, in every respect, the more convenient one. The seed should be sown in March; and as a portion often fails to germinate, it is a good precaution to use about double the quantity of seed that may be ultimately necessary. The ground should be hoed, and kept clear of weeds; and towards the end of the first summer the young plants should be thinned out to about six inches apart. A slight crop of onions, lettuce, cauliflower, or turnips may be grown between the rows during the first, and if the rows be wide, the second year also. The young heads, or stalks —the edible part—should not be cut for use before the third spring, and they are not in perfection until the fourth or fifth. Asparagus can scarcely be over-manured. The time to apply it is at the end of autumn, when the annual flower-stocks are removed. If grown in beds, their surface should be stirred with a fork, and a layer of well-rotted dung then spread over, the whole covered with a sprinkling of earth from the alleys. When the plants are grown in rows, the manure is simply dug in by means of a three-pronged fork, care being taken not to injure the roots. These operations being repeated annually, no further culture is required. If grown in beds, however, about the end of March or the beginning of April the surface is loosened with a short three-tined fork, introducing it slantingly two or three inches below the mould, and turning up the top earth near the crown of the roots, being careful not to wound them. The surface should then be raked level, lengthways, drawing off the rough earth and hard clods into the alleys. Loosening the bed in this manner enables the shoots to rise in free growth, admits the air, rain, and sunshine into the ground, and encourages the roots to produce buds of a handsome full size. The time for cutting asparagus is from about the middle of April to the middle of July. It is necessary to observe a due moderation in taking the crop, as the shoots, when much cut, become every year smaller and less valuable. Hence it is almost a general rule with gardeners never to cut asparagus after green peas have come into season. The best mode of cutting is to scrape away an inch or two of the earth from about the shoot intended to be cut, and then slip the asparagus-knife down another inch or two, taking care not to wound the crown or any other shoot. Shoots two inches under ground, and three or four above it, are generally considered to make the handsomest dishes.

A most excellent plan in preparing new beds of asparagus is—after the beds are prepared, to sow them with onions, and after that, to dibble in the asparagus seed at the usual distance, putting three or four seeds in each hole. When the plants come up, weed out the weakest, leaving only the strongest plant in each place. When taking the onions, be careful not to disturb the asparagus plants. The beds must be annually dressed as before mentioned. By this plan you have a crop of onions as well as the anticipated successive crops of asparagus.

Rhubarb (*Rheum*), a native of Asia and Tartary, was first introduced into this country in 1573. It is propagated by seed and dividing the roots. The many new and excellent varieties have so improved this plant, that stalks can be gathered from seedlings in the first year; and consequently raising from seed is now the general mode of propagating rhubarb. Sow in light deep earth, in spring, and the plants, if kept eight or nine inches asunder, will be fit for transplanting in autumn, and for use the next spring. When the roots are divided, care must be taken to retain a bud on the crown of each section; they may be planted at once where they are finally to remain. Rhubarb should always be planted in a shaded or northern situation, if the garden contains such a one, as their stems will be finer and better when not too much exposed to the sun; and as most

other plants require more light, the rhubarb occupies a
situation not appropriate for many others. A rich but
porous soil is the best. The plants should not be nearer
together than two feet every way. A dressing of well-
rotted manure should be stirred into the earth about them
every autumn. No further cultivation is necessary than
keeping the ground free from weeds, and occasionally stirring
it, during summer, with a three-pronged fork. Such a
plantation will continue good many years. The flower-
stalks should never be allowed to produce flowers. When
taking the stalks for use, remove a little earth, and bending
down the leaf you wish to remove, slip it off from the crown,
without breaking it or using a knife. The stalks are fit for
use when the leaves are half expanded; but a larger produce is obtained by letting them remain till in full expansion, as is practised by the market-gardeners. Rhubarb is
easily forced: some treat it like sea-kale, covering the roots
allowed to remain in the ground with pots or boxes, and
surrounding them with fermenting stable-litter. By taking
up the roots in November, and planting them in pots in a rich
soil, and keeping them in a dark and warm place, the stems
will be grown sufficiently to afford a supply at Christmas;
or they may be planted in rotten dung which has been previously placed in a dark cellar or shed; they will commence
growing, provided they are kept sufficiently damp. Rhubarb grown in this manner, the stalks being partially
etiolated, possesses a delicacy and flavour superior to that
grown in the open air. Not only tarts and pies, but delicious jam and jelly, as well as a good imitation of Rhenish
wine, can be produced from the rhubarb stalk.

The Artichoke (*Cynara scolymus*) is a native of the south
of Europe, and was introduced to this country in 1548. It
requires a deep, cool, dry soil; and is propagated by parting
the roots in April, the sets being planted out in rows four
or five feet asunder, and two feet apart in the rows. The
young plants generally afford a crop the first season, which

H

succeeds that of the old ones, and for this reason—in some
gardens a new plantation is made every year. During
summer, they require no other attention than to be kept
clear of weeds. In November, the decayed stems and leaves
must be removed, the ground cleared, and a litter of straw,
or the refuse of a stable-yard, to the depth of a foot, drawn
up close round the base of the leaves, in order to protect the
plant from frost. In April, this litter should be taken away,
the stools examined, and two or three only of the strongest
shoots permitted to remain; the offsets afford materials for
a young plantation. Some well-rotted dung, or fresh sea-
weed, should be dug into the ground each year, in November,
at the time of the winter dressing. In a few years these
plants degenerate; it is, therefore, a general rule not to
keep an artichoke plantation longer than four, or at the most,
six years. Scarcely any kind of grub or wire-worm ever
touches the roots of artichokes; consequently they make an
excellent preparative for a crop of onions, shalot, or garlic.

About the middle of the month Beans and Peas may be
sown in sheltered situations. To sow peas at this season of
the year, draw drills four inches deep and four feet apart;
scatter the seed of the earliest sorts regularly in the drills,
and cover with three inches of earth. If there be symptoms
of hard frost, cover the drills with about three inches in
depth of light tan or vegetable mould. When the peas have
vegetated, before they have got up to the covering, draw in
with a rake or hoe to one side of the rows; and when the
peas are coming through the ground, if the weather be
severe, the covering should again be drawn over and about
them. Where there is a close paling or a wall, standing in
an east and west position, a row of peas may be sown on the
south side of it, and if they are carefully defended from
rigorous frosts and heavy rains, and trained up against the
wall in spring, a crop of very early peas may be obtained.
Mice, by eating the seed, do great injury to the early bean
and pea crops; they are also particularly fond of, and very

destructive to, the roots of crocuses. An excellent trap for these predaceous little animals is made by half filling a pickling-jar—such as will hold two or three quarts—with water, and sinking it to the rim between the rows of peas or beans; rub a little dripping, or fat of any kind round the inside of the rim of the jar; and the trap is set and baited. It is surprising the number of mice that a few such jars will entrap in the course of a single night.

Every spare piece of ground should be dug and turned up into ridges, whenever the weather permits; but do not dig or trench when the ground is in a wet state. Take an opportunity when the ground is frozen to wheel out manure for next season's crops. Lay each barrowful in a compact heap, and cover it with a little earth; this will prevent the virtues of the manure from being exhausted by the action of the atmosphere, or washed away by heavy rains. It is not proper to let these heaps lie too long, for in that case the spots under them will be too much manured, and the intervening spaces too little; consequently the crops will grow unequally, and are often partly lost.

The year is closed, and we take leave of our Monthly Calendar of Operations. In the subsequent pages we ask the reader's attention to the instructions laid down for the perfect cultivation of the chief flowers of the garden.

PROPAGATION OF ROSES.

ROSES require a strong, loamy soil, and the deeper it is the better, if the subsoil be dry. Where the ground is not naturally rich, a quantity of rotten manure should be added to it; and, every spring, manure forked in about the plants. Roses are propagated chiefly by cuttings, layers, and buds.

Cuttings of the hardy kinds of roses, such as the hybrids of the Chinese and Bourbon, the Boursault, Ayrshire, Evergreen, Multiflora, and the Hybrid Perpetual, may be struck in the open ground. The best time is in autumn, just before the fall of the leaf. The cutting may be from nine inches to a foot in length, and should be taken off close to the old wood with what gardeners term a heel. Fig. 1 represents a cutting ready for planting, a is the heel. When the cutting is planted, two or three eyes should be left above the ground. If you have a quantity, they may be inserted about an inch apart, and a few small boughs, or fern fronds, stuck in amongst them, as a shelter from sun and frost. In

spring, those that have not struck root should be pulled out;
and in autumn, those which have succeeded may be transplanted to where it is intended they are to flower. Cuttings
of the more tender kinds—as the Bourbon, Noisette, Chinese,
and Tea-scented, should be placed under a hand-glass. The
glass should be occasionally lifted on fine days, to admit air
and dry the soil; any decayed leaves or cuttings should at

Fig. 1.

such times be removed; water will seldom be required till
the spring. About April these cuttings will have rooted;
they should then be taken up, potted singly, and removed
to a frame, or a close shaded room, for a few days. Such as
are intended to be grown in the open air should be planted
out in May. Roses grown as dwarfs, or bushes, are the
kinds most generally layered. The soil about the plant
should first be loosened; then, selecting a good shoot, strip
off a few leaves at a distance, varying from six inches to two
feet from the point of the shoot (see fig. 2, *a a*); then, taking
the shoot in the left hand, insert a sharp knife just behind
an eye, at *b*, on the upper side of the shoot, and pass it

evenly and carefully upwards, cutting about half through
the shoot, and for an inch and a half or two inches in length.
Bend down the shoot, so that you may see the proper place
to bury it; then open a hole, press the shoot into it, peg it
down two or three inches beneath the surface, and cover
with the soil. It is well to twist the shoot a little after the
cut is made, so that the end of the tongue, b, from which
the roots will be emitted, may have a downward direction
when in the ground. It is also a good plan to split the
tongue, and keep the split open by inserting a small stone

Fig. 2.

in it. Each layer should be tied to a small stake, c, to prevent its being agitated by the wind. June, July, and
August, are the best months for layering; if the weather be
dry, the layers should be watered. About November they
will be ready to be taken from the parent plants, by cutting
them off within two inches from the tongue; then transplant
them to wherever they are intended to flower. In spring
they should be pruned down to three or four eyes: some of
them will bloom the same summer or autumn. Standard
roses are well-known ornaments of the garden; they look
well in any position, but appear to the greatest advantage
when planted in opposite lines in the centre of

two beds, one on each side of a central or principal walk. In pruning, the young shoots should be annually shortened to about two or three inches from the point they started from; and if the head should become too large and straggling, some of the old wood should be cut out, and its place supplied by young shoots, which spring from the centre; keeping in view, as you prune, that the beauty of a standard consists principally in its having a round compact head, so

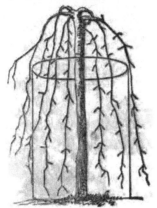

Fig. 3.

as to present a favourable appearance when seen from any side. Weeping roses form beautiful objects when planted singly on lawns; they are roses of a pendulous habit, such as the Ayrshire and Evergreen, budded on stocks four feet and upwards in height. The main shoots ought not to be shortened, after the second year, until they reach the earth; prune the laterals only, and flowers will be produced all along the branches from the head to the ground. When they attain their full size, a hoop, as in fig. 3, should be attached, to prevent the branches being injured by the wind. Fig. 3 represents a weeping rose of full growth, without leaves, to show how it should be trained and pruned.

THE RANUNCULUS.

The Ranunculus is closely associated with that queer passage in human history, Florimania. It is one of the flowers that used to drive men mad, and with the Tulip, the Anemone, and the Dahlia, has played some strange part in those scenes of excitement which we are wont to associate

with South Sea Bubbles and commercial crises. It has, indeed, a strange history; though, as exhibiting the possibilities of human folly, the Tulip leaves it far behind. Now that florimania has given place to a healthy love of flowers and honest modes of trading in them, the Ranunculus reasserts its claims, and a dazzling spectacle is a bed of the florist's varieties well-bloomed and arranged in tasteful contrasts. This flower is especially a pet of the fancier, for it has as high exhibitional qualities as any; we have it now thoroughly double, beautifully spherical, so as to form two-thirds of a ball, the outline exactly spherical, the petals laid regularly one upon the other, and every tint marked with precision; in fact, the colours are as decisive as if printed, and the forms as perfect as if turned out by machinery—a triumph of patient culture and careful cross-breeding.

The Ranunculus is a member of the celebrated family of the Buttercups, and, like its kindred, it loves a deep mellow loam, plenty of moisture while growing, and a free pure air. The true florist's varieties require and deserve great care, but the inferior kinds grown in the borders do well with the treatment given to the generality of hardy perennials. The Turbans are the best for border culture, and are exceedingly showy.

The proper soil for choice Ranunculuses is a rich mellow loam; the proper manure, well-rotted cow or horse dung; recent manure ruins it, so do any exciting compounds of night-soil, blood, or chemical stimulants, or an excess of manure of any kind, all which have been recommended and the proportions stated with ridiculous precision. If the soil of the garden is at all suitable, manure it well in preference to preparing composts; if it is not of a loamy and somewhat crumbly character, procure the top spit of an old meadow, one in which buttercups abound is best; ridge it up, turning it occasionally for about six months, and with this and some well-rotted dung prepare your bed.

In preparing the bed, rake out the old soil to a depth of fifteen inches; then lay down rotten cow-dung two inches thick; work up the old sweetened soil well with half its quantity of decayed stable and cow dung, and with this fill it up, and then edge it either with some low-growing edging plant, or Hogg's edging tiles, which have the effect of an elegant stone moulding, with the advantage of being easily removed in altering a bed.

An amateur desirous of a good bed of Ranunculuses, but not aiming at the production of show flowers, might make sure or a good display by properly planting them in well-manured loam, in a *firm state*, and if prepared three months before planting all the better. The roots of the Ranunculus always work deep, hence a shallow soil is quite unsuitable. A depth of three feet is none too much, and if the lower spit s a sound loam the roots will reach it and frequent watering will be less necessary. In a heavy soil a little sand may be added with advantage, but a slight admixture will be enough.

The Ranunculus bed ought to be ready early in January, and the best time for planting is between the 1st and 20th of February, the precise day or week being determined by the weather. There has been a good deal of discussion as to the proper planting season; but it is now pretty generally agreed that autumn planting is attended with risk, for which early blooming is the only compensation, and that the first twenty days of February are the safest for collections of any value. In cold, wet, and very tenacious soils, or in exposed situations, it would be better to defer planting till the first week in March; and planting may be more safely deferred in the Ranunculus than with most other tubers, for they retain their vitality out of the ground two or three years, and if kept cool and dry, suffer but little exhaustion by delay.

The best mode of planting Ranunculuses is to drill them, and the operation is performed as follows:—Choose a fine day, have your tubers sorted as you mean to plant them, and your zinc or wooden tallies ready. You have already planned how the colours and sorts are to be arranged, and have entered in your note-book all necessary heads, so that when you begin planting you will have to work only and not to consider.

First, rake the soil so as to give the bed a gentle convexity; then put down the line for the first row, and with a small-pointed hoe, or the corner of a common one, draw the drill exactly two inches deep. The orthodox depth is an inch and a half, but I prefer, and therefore recommend, a trifle deeper, on the principle of giving free work before the foliage appears, as well as to escape as much as possible the effects of the very late frosts to which we have been subject for some years past.

Into the drill sprinkle a very little fine sand, then proceed according to your book, and plant the first row of tubers, inserting the proper label *at once*, not trusting to memory one jot. Each tuber must be gently pressed into the soil to about half the length of the claws, care being taken that none of the claws are broken in the process. The drills may be five inches apart, and the roots four inches apart, in the drills, though some growers prefer six or even eight inches every way.

When the drills are filled and tallied, sprinkle a little sand over the tubers, and then neatly rake down the soil over them, and dress up the bed as you intend it to remain.

When the young foliage begins to show itself, the bed should be carefully trod over between the rows, firmness of the soil being a prime element of success in the general cultivation. If the weather is dry, they may be watered night and morning, and if the soil has not been so liberally manured as it should, weak manure-water may be used. The Ranunculus likes a moist soil; nevertheless, it is a mistaken notion to water it either frequently or copiously. Artificial watering never does as much good as is expected of it, and if it can be dispensed with it is all the better for the plants. It is a good plan to mulch the beds with moss. or old tan, or even old and well-sweetened dung, placing the dressing neatly about the rows. Such a procedure will frequently obviate the necessity of watering, and carry the plants through till rain comes.

As soon as the plants have done flowering, remove the flower stems, and when the foliage begins to turn yellow take up the tubers, dry them in the shade slowly, and store away in a dry, cool place till the planting season comes round again. In "Garden Favourites and Exhibition Flowers," the lover of the Ranunculus will find a list of about a hundred and fifty of the choicest kinds, from which a selection may be made so as to comprise all the various colours and varieties of markings which are indeed beautiful. The principal professional grower is Tysoe, of Wallingford, and to him we are indebted for an immense number of seedlings of the highest order of merit.

THE DAHLIA.

Dahlias do not require too rich a soil—except those intended for exhibition, or show flowers, the management of which we shall treat of presently—in very nutritious ground they exhaust their vigour in producing strong stems and leaves, thereby causing the flowers to be poor, ill-formed, and few in number. A very barren, light soil, is equally unsuitable, and should be strengthened by a judicious addition of leaf-mould before the plants are placed in it. Where the soil is wet, heavy, clay land—the most unsuitable of all—it must be rendered friable by an admixture of drift, or river sand, or, what is still better, road-scrapings. About November, the sand or scrapings should be laid over the soil to the depth of two inches, and well dug in, the ground being left rough through the winter; in spring two more inches should be laid over, and dug in as before. A moderately rich, light loam, is indisputably the best soil; but it must be borne in mind that this plant exhausts the ground to a remarkable degree, and consequently will not succeed, if grown too frequently on the same spot. A clear, open situation, freely exposed to the sun, without either shade or shelter, is indispensable for the production of fine blossoms. Those who have but limited space and few plants, should place them singly, or otherwise, in the situa-

tions most advantageous for cultivation and display which
their ground affords. No general directions can apply to
particular localities. But where there is plenty of room,
and a large collection of plants, no mode of growing the
dahlia has such an imposing effect as when planted in a
mass by themselves, unmixed with any other flower. When
planting in a mass, two important objects must be kept in
view, or else the effect will be spoiled. The first is to place
the plants according to their respective heights ; the second
is to associate them so that their colours may harmonis,
agreeably. If the clump is to be on a border backed by a
wall or hedge, so that it can be seen only from one side, the
tallest growing plants must be placed in the rear ; the next
tallest in front of those, and so down to the shortest, which
must hold the front rank of all. But if the clump is to be
formed on a bed which can be viewed from all sides, the
tallest must be placed in the centre, and the next in height
successively downwards, till the shortest are placed in the
front. To harmonise the colours—purples and crimsons,
and crimsons and scarlets, should be separated by yellow,
white, or buff ; the salmon-coloured and buff separated by
white. The plants should be placed three feet from each
other every way ; this space will keep each plant sufficiently
distinct when close to them, and yet so united, that at a
short distance the whole clump will appear as a solid mass ;
it also affords room to get amongst and attend to the plants.
Another mode of planting dahlias, which exhibits a grand
effect, is to place a row on each side of a walk as an avenue ;
in such position the plants need not be more than two and
a-half feet apart.

Dahlias are propagated by dividing the tubers when they
have formed incipient shoots, by seed, and by cuttings. As
the last method is comparatively useless to the amateur we
shall not take up space to describe it, but proceed to the
first two. The roots—or more properly speaking, the
tubers—should be kept cool, inactive, and entire, until the

beginning of May, when they should be planted out in the open border, barely buried in the soil, and covered with a hand-glass. The eyes of the tubers will soon push forth young shoots, and when these have attained the length of two or three inches, the tuber should be cut with a sharp knife, so as to retain a portion of the tuber attached to each shoot. These young plants may be placed in pots with light soil, and kept in the house for a short time; or they may at once be planted in the borders where they are to flower, sheltering them from the sun by day, and from cold at night, until they are established. Another method, slightly different indeed, is to place the roots in a warm situation—a south border, for instance—covering them all but their eyes with rotten bark, leaf-mould, or other light material; when the buds break, divide as before described. It is a safe plan when dividing the roots, to cut so as to secure, if possible, more than one promising bud on each piece. It is satisfactory to know, that except in florists' gardens and large establishments, where quantities of plants are required early in the season, artificial heat is not required for propagating the dahlia from the tuber. We have the high authority of Paxton for saying, that plants raised according to these methods frequently grow stronger and flower better than those which have been raised earlier in the season by the application of heat.

When the young plants, by whatever mode obtained, are finally planted out where they are intended to flower, the upper part of the root should not be less than three inches beneath the surface, and the soil should be carefully settled down about the roots, by gently pouring in water as the hole is being filled up. A large-size flower-pot inverted over the young plant makes an excellent protection at night; and shade may be afforded in the day time, by branches of fir or laurel stuck in the ground. A stake, suitable to the full height of the flower, must be inserted and fixed firmly into the ground close to the stem, at the time of planting. This is imperatively necessary; for the insertion of the stake after planting is sure to injure the roots, check the growth of the plant, and destroy its beauty. The leading shoot, as it advances, must be tied to the stake with strips of bass. These bands must not in the first instance be tied too tight, and frequent attention must be given to see that they do not hinder the stem from swelling to its full size. During the whole period of growth, the soil about the roots should be kept moderately moist, but not over-drenched with water, which to this plant is equally as injurious as drought. If the soil be light, and the summer excessively dry and hot, a layer of fresh cow manure for about two feet round the base of the stem of the plant is highly recommended as a preventative to too rapid evaporation.

Some train dahlias in the espalier form, by permitting three or four stems to grow from each root, laying them diagonally on both sides, and filling up the centre with the lateral shoots. Another mode of training is to peg them down so as to cover a bed. The bed being prepared, the number of plants required to cover it is to be deduced from their respective heights, for they must be placed at such distances from each other as will allow the extremities of the branches of each plant to cover the whole of the stem of its next neighbour; so that the bed, when at full growth, may present one uniform mass of foliage and flowers. The plants should not have more than one or two stems, which, at the time of planting, are secured to the ground by a hooked peg; the branches which proceed from these stems must be pegged down also, as the plant advances in growth, and until the bed be covered. After all, there is no system of training so simple, so secure, so well adapted to the natural habits of the dahlia, and so eligible for displaying its flowers, as that of reducing it to a single stem, and fastening it to a single stake.

Having described the culture of the Dahlia, from the tuber to the flower, we shall now turn to its most interesting mode of propagation. It is from the seed alone that all new varieties are obtained, and it is only from the seed that the plant has been, and no doubt will be, so greatly improved. Animals domesticated by man, in course of time, though they may retain their original forms and distinctive features, yet vary in colour, not only from their wild relations of the woods and fields, but even from one another. The rabbit, duck, and pigeon, are familiar instances of this well-known law of nature, which extends also to the vegetable kingdom. We have seen, in the early part of this paper, that the dahlia, at its first introduction, was rather shy in running into varieties ; now, it is so liable to *sport*, as gar-

WILD DAHLIA.

deners term it, that dark and light crimson, dark and light scarlet, salmon-colour, lilac, dark purple, and striped flowers, have all been obtained from the seed of one single head of florets ! What an interesting field of experimental adventure this simple fact discloses to the amateur florist ! About the middle or end of January, the seeds should be sown in shallow pans placed in a hotbed frame, near the glass, and exposed to the light; as soon as the seed-leaves are properly developed, the young plants should be pricked out into other pans, at the distance of an inch from each other ; they should then be watered, and shaded for a few days until they recover the shock of this, their first removal, and are briskly thriving again. When they have attained the height of two inches, they should be potted, singly, into small pots, and gradually inured to a lower temperature. As they increase in size, they require to be shifted into larger pots, and advantage taken of all opportunities of hardening them for the open air. In short, the process is

CULTIVATED DAHLIA.

just the same as that previously described for raising half-hardy annuals. The seedlings may be planted out in the open air about the end of May, and the course of culture already detailed must be followed. Until the seedlings show their flowers there are no means of ascertaining, with certainty, their quality or colour; though it has been

observed, that plants with wholly green stems produce white
flowers, those with brownish stems the darker coloured
flowers, and those with light-coloured stems, pale or blush-
coloured flowers. When the blooming season arrives, the
seedlings should be examined early each morning before the
sun has shone upon the flowers, as their true colours are
better ascertained at that time of day.

Such plants as are considered unworthy of preservation
should be at once pulled up and thrown away, for they will
only exhaust the soil to no purpose; and those which, having proved good, are worthy to be retained, should not be
suffered to bloom profusely, in order that the tubers may
retain more nutritive matter, and thereby be better able to
produce strong and healthy plants in the following season.
The tubers must never be subjected to the destructive
influence of frost. About the end of September, some
ashes, saw-dust, pease-haulm, or other protective materials,
should be laid over the roots; and when the stems and
leaves turn black, the plant should be cut down to within
six inches of the ground. A few days afterwards, taking
advantage of a fine morning, the tubers must be lifted, and
laid exposed to the sun during the remainder of the day.
When the soil about the roots is dry, all that can be removed
without injury should be taken off. The tubers may then
be buried in dry sand, or laid on a shelf or boarded floor
where they will be perfectly free from frost and damp, and
in a moderately cool temperature, being at no time through
the winter higher than 45°, nor lower than 36°.

Properties of the Dahlia.

1. The flower should be a perfect circle when viewed in
front, the petals should be broad at the ends, smooth at the
edges, thick in substance, perfectly free from indenture or
point, stiff to hold its form; it should cup a little, but not
enough to show the under surface. They should be in

regular rows, forming an outline of a perfect circle, without
any vacancy between them, and all in the circle should be
the same size, uniformly opened to the same shape, and
not crumpled.

2. The flower should form two-thirds of a ball when
looked at sideways. The rows of petals should rise one
above another symmetrically; every petal should cover the
join of the two petals under it—what the florists call imbri-
cating—by which means the circular appearance is preserved throughout.

3. The centre should be perfect, the unbloomed petals
lying with their points towards the centre should form a
button, and should be the highest part of the flower—com-
pleting the ball.

4. The flower should be symmetrical. The petals should
open boldly, without showing their underside, even when
half opened, and should form circular rows, uniformly laid,
evenly opened, and enlarging by degrees to the outer row
of all.

5. The flower should be very double. The rows of petals
lying one above another, should cover one another very
nearly; not more should be seen in depth than half the
breadth; the more they are covered so as to leave them distinct, the better in that respect; the petals, therefore,
though cupped, must be shallow.

6. The size of the flower, when well grown, should be not
less than four inches in diameter, and not more than six.

7. The colour should be dense, whatever it be; not as if
it were a white dipped in colour, but as if the whole flower
were coloured throughout. Whether tipped or edged, it
must be free from splashes and blotches, or indefinite marks
of any kind; and new flowers—unless they beat all old
ones of the same colour, or are of a novel colour themselves,
with a majority of the points of excellence—should be re-
jected.

If the petals show the underside too much, even when

Mr. Groom, of Clapham, one of the first tulip-growers in the world, and who, no doubt, possesses the best collection extant—the Dutch having completely lost their pre-eminence in the finer varieties—cultivates these plants in beds of four feet in width. When the bed is ready to receive the bulbs, its surface is brought to an accurate convex curve by means of a piece of board, in the required form, termed a strike. This being done, the places of each and every bulb are exactly marked by the same implement, which is divided into eight spaces of six inches each. On the flat side of the strike, at the marks between the spaces, are small staples which receive seven small pegs; these, when the strike is laid across the bed, mark the places for one row of bulbs. From this first row, which is six inches from one end of the bed, six inches are measured at each side, and the strike being again laid over the bed at the termination of these measurements, gives the places of the plants in the next row —the same method being continued till every place is accurately determined. From the foregoing, it will be seen that there are seven bulbs in each row across the bed; that each bulb is six inches apart, every way, from another; and that the side and end ones are six inches from the edge of the bed—the length of the bed depending upon the number of bulbs the grower possesses, or chooses to plant in it; a bed twenty-five feet in length is said to have the most brilliant effect. The places for the bulbs having been thus found, a little clean sand should be sprinkled on each position, the bulb placed on it, and a little very sandy earth put over, so as to envelope each bulb in a cone. The bed should then be covered with a sound, fresh loam, and the surface smoothed off with the back of the strike, which for this purpose is formed with a curve and shoulders; the former taking in the breadth of the bed, while the latter slides against boards placed at each side; the whole moved onwards, takes off the redundant soil, leaving the surface regularly rounded, the centre being six inches higher than at the sides. The tallest-growing flowers must be placed in the centre; the nearest in size next, and so decreasing in height, the shortest are placed at the sides. The convexity of surface permits the bulbs to be covered with a depth of soil proportionate to the size of the plant. No tulip bulb, however strong the plant may be, should be covered by more than four inches of soil, measuring from its upper part; nor should it be buried less than two inches, however small or weak it may be.

It is a most important object to arrange the bulbs in the bed, so that when in bloom the plants will make the greatest possible display.

If symptoms of frost appear after the bulbs are planted, the bed must be covered with fern, straw, or other similar protection; for though the tulip can scarcely be destroyed by the most rigorous frost known in this climate, yet a short exposure to even a slight congelation will injure the bulb, and its effects will be plainly apparent in the blooming season by the split discoloured sepals, and other imperfections of the flower. When the plants appear above ground, the protecting material must be removed, the surface of the soil slightly stirred, and a covering of hoops and mats, or waterproof transparent cloth, which is much better, placed over the bed, as heavy rain, hail, or frost, are equally injurious; air and light, however, must be freely admitted on all favourable occasions. In March, the bed should be again stirred, and the soil drawn close to the stems of the plants. The covering should be removed on fine days only, until about the latter end of April, when it must be taken away altogether to make room for the top-cloth, or awning, which should then be erected over the bed. A cheap and simple awning, consisting of a few uprights and rafters, and a piece of canvass, may be erected by any one possessing the minutest development of the organ of constructiveness; the subjoined figure, which we trust requires but little explanation, is intended to represent an economical awning.

The canvass is fastened along the ridge *a a*, and should be

long enough to reach down to the ground.   A roller, *b b*, is
fixed to the lower edge of the canvass, and a cord attached to

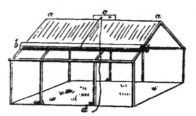

AN ECONOMICAL AWNING.

the ridge is brought down under the canvass, round the
roller, and up over the canvass to a pulley at *c;* so that by
pulling or slackening the cord *d*, the canvass is rolled up or
let down.   On the other side of the frame there is also
another cord, canvass, roller, and pulley, used in the same
manner, and for the same purpose.   The blooming season
draws on apace in May, and from the moment that the
flowers commence to show colour, neither sunshine nor rain
must be allowed to fall upon them.   Still, a free circulation
of air must be constantly kept up, and therefore the canvass
should not be let down close to the ground except in windy
weather, which is exceedingly prejudicial to the flowers;
then the canvass should be let down close on the windy
side.   If any bulbs have perished, or failed to produce bloom
—a great eyesore in a bed—the deficiency may be supplied
by transplanting others with the *transplanter*.

During the time that the flowers are in bloom, each one
should be particularly examined, tulip-book in hand, and
memoranda made according to their individual and general
appearance.   As soon as the bloom commences to fade, the
awning should be removed, and the plants exposed to the
full influence of the sun and air.   When the sepals drop,
the seed-pods should be picked off; and about the end of
June, or beginning of July, when the foliage has turned

yellow and shrivelled, the bulbs may be taken up, the offsets separated from them, and the stems cut off with a sharp
knife, about half an inch from the bulbs, and the latter
put in drawers placed in the shade, there to dry and
harden.

In August the bulbs should be cleaned free from dirt;
their skins and the bit of stem adhering to them taken
away; each one placed in its own division of the drawer,
and the drawers placed in the cabinet. About this time,
too, the compost should be thrown out of the bed, and the
fresh compost for next season carefully turned over and
searched for those destructive pests the wire-worm and
grub. In September the bed may be planned and arranged

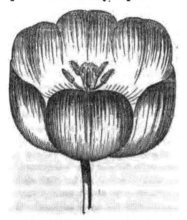

TULIPA GESNERIANA.

in the drawers. In October the offsets should be planted
out in the reserve-garden. Choose a dry, airy situation;
the soil should be fresh sandy loam, with a little rotten cow
manure placed from seven to twelve inches beneath the
surface. The beds should be raised six or eight inches

above the alleys, formed rather convex on the surface, and provided with hoops and mats, to use as occasion may require, as protection from heavy rains, hail, and frost. Tulips never require to be artificially watered, even in the driest seasons, at any period from planting to taking up. At the same time moderate, gentle showers in spring, before the flowers appear, are most beneficial to the plants, and at such times the covers should be removed.

The tyro, when purchasing bulbs, should select those that have not lost the brown skin—are not mouldy nor soft at the root end, and are full, solid, and rather pointed at the other.

THE SWEET-WILLIAM.

This universal favourite belongs to the same race of plants as the pink and carnation. If there is anything in a name, it has some advantage in regard to its family designation "Dianthus"—the divine flower; *Dianthus barbatus* being the botanic name of the Sweet-William. It is a biennial or triennial, but best grown as biennial, the seed being sown one year to bloom the next. "It is," says Cobbett, "one of the most ornamental plants of the garden, an oblong bed of Sweet-Williams being, to my eye, the most beautiful thing that one can behold of the flower kind. The varieties of colour are without end, and the stiff stalk of the plant holds them up to view in so complete a manner that there is nothing left to wish for in this plant. The seed should be sown in an open bed in the spring, and in rows, which should be kept hoed and weeded through the summer. In autumn plant them out where they are to blow, and do not put the plants nearer than within six inches of one another, either in beds or in clumps. If you wish to propagate a particular plant, you must do it by striking a cutting from one of the flower-stalks; but this should be before that stalk has flowered. Let there be two joints to the cutting; and strike it under a hand-glass upon a little heat."

This flower, like so many others, has of late years been greatly improved by careful cultivation, and flowers of such large size and magnificent colours have been produced, that the original, beautiful as it is, can scarcely be recognised in the cultivated and highly-developed flower.

THE PANSY AND ITS CULTURE.

A Pansy grown according to the orthodox pattern has a perfect roundness of form, the entire flower representing a circle. Where the petals cover each other, the indentation in the outline should be scarcely or not at all perceptible, the petals should have great breadth, should be fleshy in substance, quite flat, and with no irregularities on the margin, a single notch being sufficient to ruin a flower, whatever its excellences of outline and colour. The ground colour should be decided, and any markings on the ground should be quite regular, and especially those which radiate from the centre. The eye should be dark, and a velvet softness should overspread the whole, not only to the eye, but to the touch.

So far as to the named varieties; of the unnamed the sorts are numberless, and the better kinds of them are the worn-out offspring of sorts that have had their day; many of them still very beautiful, and worth the culture of any lover of flowers who does not care to expend money and time on the study of novelties and changes of fashion. That is just one of the advantages of pansy-growing, that a poor flower which has lost its name and title to homage is still beautiful, and may embellish the border, without fear of being treated with contempt.

As the pansy during the summer season flowers a few weeks after sowing, a succession may be easily obtained from carefully-saved seed. If required to bloom the same year, the seed should be sown from February to May, and the plants bedded out in succession as soon as they have half-a-dozen strong leaves each. The early sowings should be in pans filled with rich sandy loam, and forwarded by gentle heat; the late sowings may be made in the open air, and, if the weather should be dry, water should be liberally administered, and shade given during hot sunny weather. Moderate shade, good drainage, a plentiful supply of water and a generous compost of old cow-dung, sand, and leaf-mould, or loam, are the requisites for producing good pansies, and the seedlings must be bedded out with such combined advantages, or the best sorts will soon run false.

The next mode of bedding out is as follows: Choose a sunny quarter which you can shade when necessary; prepare it by first securing a free drainage; for, though the pansy delights in moisture, damp soon destroys it. Cut a trench a foot wide and a foot deep, and throw into the trench about three inches of sharp sand or Thames grit, and upon the sand lay seven or eight inches of well-rotted cow-dung, or a mixture of well-rotted stable-dung and leaf-mould. Tread this down firmly, and fill up the trench with mellow loam, in which a good proportion of sand or virgin earth from a meadow has been mingled. The whole should be sweet and well pulverised, and neatly dressed up before planting. Set your plants out along the trench, carefully spreading out the fibres of the roots and placing a little rotted dung in each hole, but so that the roots must grow a little to reach it.

THE COMMON PANSY.   The same flower improved by cultivation.

Dress up with care, and water liberally, and give shade if the weather be bright. The plants will soon take root and show signs of progress, but all will be spoilt if left to the risk of dry weather, and exposure to sun and insufficient nourishment.

Now, if such a collection consists of named sorts for which you have paid a good price, you must carefully watch the first blooms that show, and destroy or give away every plant that appears deficient in character.. Whatever its colours and special qualities, it must conform to the accepted "properties" of a florist's pansy, and all your courage must be exercised to extinguish or remove blemished specimens.

If you design to raise new sorts by hybridization, or to exhibit any which appear worthy of it, you must adopt the practice of pinching off the flower-buds as they appear, leaving only one or two, or but a small proportion of the whole, to open bloom. This plan will increase the size and vigour of the few flowers that remain, and if by this practice you succeed in bringing a few to high perfection of form, colour, and size, you must propagate at once from cuttings, for fear that accident should rob you of the chance of getting seed. This is the more necessary as the pansy rarely yields more than one fine set of blooms, and these are apt to lose their distinctive features unless the sort be perpetuated by means of cuttings.

In May, June, and July, the cuttings are to be taken from such plants as appear most worth propagating. They should be taken from young and vigorous plants before they have exhausted themselves by free blooming. Pinch them off as cleanly as possible each cutting two inches long; cut off all the stem below the joint, and as close to the joint as possible; remove the lower leaves, and dibble them in by means of the finger or a skewer, in rich sandy loam, covering with a hand-glass. It is best to press the hand-glass on the soil first, so as to mark it, and then the cuttings may be placed regularly inside the mark. A new pot has lately come into use: it is made with a rim, on which a hand-glass fits, and is admirably adapted for striking cuttings of all kinds, but particularly of pansies. They are to be obtained in Covent Garden, and should be in the possession of every pansy-grower.

After one good watering, it will be well to keep the cuttings only moderately moist; and if much exhalation condenses on the glass, lift it off for half an hour in the morning, and, after wiping it dry, replace it before the sun reaches the border. In six or seven weeks, or even earlier sometimes, the plants will be in a proper condition for planting out, and may be bedded for blooming, either in beds by themselves, carefully arranged as to colours, or in the borders with other flowers. In either case their character can be sustained only by following the plan we have already described. Shake the earth from their roots, and replant them with care, so that they will have to push out their fibres in order to reach the manure; a good proportion of sand must be used in the compost, the plants carefully shaded until they make root, and water abundantly supplied.

In transplanting purchased roots that have begun to bloom, it is necessary to remove the ball of clay with which the roots are generally crushed up, and wash the fibres quite clean, but without breaking them. Then nip off every flower, and also any superabundant shoots, and plant as before directed, giving plenty of water and shading them from the sun. If the sorts are good, the cuttings may be struck in pots, under hand-glasses, or in a shady border similarly covered, and new plants obtained to succeed those already in bloom. It is most essential that the soil should be in good heart, well sweetened and pulverised, and the manure well rotted. New dung would ruin the strongest or the weakest pansy that was ever grown, and, except in very practised hands, manure-water would be equally injurious.

As the season closes, prepare your wintering quarters for those sown in August and September; for these, properly treated, will come in early in the following spring. The pansy is very hardy, but susceptible of damp; and, though fond of moisture, it soon rots under improper treatment. If they are to be wintered out of doors in beds, set them in rows nine inches apart from row to row, and five inches from plant to plant, on a south border previously prepared with proper soil, but by no means so rich as you would use in spring; your object being to harden the plants and check rather than promote growth. The choicer kinds should be potted and set in a cool greenhouse or cold pit for the winter, or if you have no such convenience, the window of an attic or dwelling-room, that window being preferable where they will be free from dust and sudden alterations of temperature. Sorts that have cost much money or great labour, should (if worth their cost) be preserved in duplicate, for fear the variety should vanish altogether, as was the case with Mr. Rogers's " Goliah," the finest pansy ever grown, but which perished after producing only one flower. If anything of a striking character shows itself in your stock, as will frequently happen in a collection of well-grown seedlings, get one or two cuttings as soon as possible, and allow but a few blooms to expand, and then tend with all care till you have secured seed.

Early spring blooms may be very well obtained from cuttings struck in August; and if you have a goodly number of August and September plants, you may secure a succession until the May plants come in, and keep up the show through autumn. I have had a gay show of pansies in the second week of February, by securing strong autumn plants from cuttings; and these, if free-blooming cuts, will continue until the spring seedlings take their place, to be again succeeded by May seedlings and cuttings. If you have any difficulty in getting cuttings from a choice sort that deserves propagation, cut the plant over and make a cutting of the main stem, carefully removing every flower-bud so as to promote a fresh growth from the root. This plan never fails if adopted in time; but if you suffer your plants to expend their strength in blooming, you may soon lose the whole collection.

Some of the best sorts ever raised have come by chance, or perhaps we should say, that that best of florists' friends, the bee, made them. Florists usually select their plants for seeding with great care, and bring together the finest plants of opposite characters ; or if some sorts have richness of odour but irregularity of form, they seek to improve them by crossing with better-formed flowers, the colours of which may perhaps be less perfect. If the grower does not care to destroy inferior, he should remove them to a safe distance from his choicer kinds.

It is a very easy matter to lose pansy seed just as it ripens ; and to prevent such a calamity, it is usual to tie a piece of gauze over the pods when they are about half ripe.

The pansy has many enemies. The grower is often the worst of them, and many collections have been lost through bad treatment. Recent manure is always injurious, and damp is generally fatal. There is so little woody fibre in the pansy, that its succulent stems soon show exhaustion if exposed to heat and drought; and, on the other hand, readily rot, if moisture stagnates above the roots. Slugs and snails are very partial to the juicy stems and tender leaves, and frequently commit sad havoc by eating the unexpanded flower from within the bud. These pests should be made scarce by a daily visit to the beds—it is the early bird that finds the worm, and the early florist may overtake many a bloated snail on his way to his burrow by an inspection of his pansies at day-break. Fresh cabbage-leaves, tiles, with pieces of carrot or apple under them, are good traps, and, if laid overnight in the neighbourhood of the plants you wish to protect, will not only attract the snails, and prevent them eating into the hearts of favourite flowers, but enable you to capture them before they retire for the day.

As this is the season for the pansy-grower to be vigilant, we commend the lovers of this established favourite to select only such sorts as have the most distinguished characters, and to have nothing to do with intermediates, or with blotched or wrinkled specimens, except as common border-flowers, at a few pence per dozen.

K

THE GENISTA.

To deal fairly by flowers, with a view to render their culture easy to those who love them, one must occasionally chat about them at seasons which, at first thought, may appear very unbefitting. For instance, who, except the

regular plodding amateur or serious nurseryman, cares about Genistas now? Folks buy them in spring through falling in love with their golden ringlets; for at Covent Garden and other such places they come out grand in very golden masses, and tempt many a one to carry home a plant for the

window, which, as soon as its bloom is over, is thrust aside
anywhere, and at last gets *nowhere*—that is, it perishes for
want of care. Now, though this sort of thing keeps trade
going, a public writer feels it incumbent upon him to im-
plore his readers not to treat any plant in a scurvy way
because it is no longer attractive. If it *has* had its day,
still cherish it, for its season will return. You yourself,
dear reader, when your youth is fled, would not like to be
kicked out of house and home; but for you youth returns
not: when once the rosy cheek gets pale and wrinkled,
restoration is forbidden by that stern leveller, Old Time,
who nips our bloom once and for ever; but restores the
bloom of flowers ever year, just to show that they ought
always to be cared for.

Now, just look to those Genistas and early Pelargoniums
and Cinerarias—what have you done with them? They
made a brave show in your windows months ago, when
flowers were scarce; and now that you have Hydranges,
and Fuchsias, and Stocks, and those abominable Tom Thumbs
that elbow every good thing aside, you don't care a fig
about your spring pets. Let me tell you, the pleasure of a
few flowers is increased tenfold when you remember that it
is by your own care that they have been produced; therefore, for the sake of having flowers of your own when spring
comes once more, *do* hunt up the Genistas—see if life is left
in them, and henceforth tend them as we shall direct, for
this is the very season to make twenty nice young plants
out of every old one that has flowered and been cast aside.

There are many species of Genista in cultivation, but the
kind which is sold so largely in the spring is *G. canariensis*,
a neat, free-flowering, very interesting plant, which, though
strictly belonging to the greenhouse, may be managed by
any one who possesses no such structure; for it is the most
accommodating greenhouse perennial we possess—more so
even than a geranium.

The Genista is a broom or a laburnum, which you please,

for brooms and laburnums are close relatives, and all the
species are favourites. The old story of the broom being
worn in battle by the founder of the Plantagenet family—
who are so called from *Planta genista*, the old name of the
broom—is a pretty jotting in the memorabilia of field
flowers; and, if historical botany were the theme, the
Genista would be just the thing to set one trotting off to
Spenser and Shakespeare for a hundred pretty readings, and
to old herbals and chronicles for many a good anecdote. But
as the culture most concerns us, it should be stated here that
the Genista numbers about sixty species known to gardeners,
and of these the best greenhouse kinds are *G. canariensis*,
Rodophna, *Racemosa*, and *Umbellata*—the first is the Genista
par excellence, a plant much grown, but not at all petted.
If its merits were rightly estimated, gardeners would by
this time have produced some good hybrids to bloom all the
summer long; such a thing would be a welcome addition to
our yellow bedding plants. *G. Atleeana*, represented in the
figure, is a hybrid raised by Mr. Atlee some years since; its
habit is dense and symmetrical; it flowers freely, and
forms, when well-grown, a graceful bush of eight or ten feet
high.

Among the hardy Genistas, those of our own moors are
really beautiful things. The one which blooms so gaily in
spring, forming a bright green dwarf bush, is *G. angelica :*
another, used in dyeing, found on most of the wastes near
London, is *G. tinctoria*, and is a first-rate plant for a rockery,
on account of the ease with which it may be trained down,
and the gaiety of its blossoms. *G. triqueta* and *G. trian-
gularis* are two other hardy sorts for the garden, that make
a splendid show in early summer. *Triqueta* is the best
indeed of the hardy sorts, and may be grown as a standard,
if worked on the laburnum stock; it is then a most graceful
ornament to a lawn.

In the cultivation of the tender kinds, a soil of peat and
loam is the best; they will not do in common garden mould,

nor do they require such frequent shifting as most other greenhouse plants. Supposing that you have a plant or so of any of the tender species; as soon as you have read this, prepare to strike some cuttings. At this time of year almost anything will strike out of doors, and the way to strike Genistas is, to set apart a little space in a shady corner, free from slugs. There make a little bed of peat, and loam, and silver-sand in equal proportions, and spread an inch of pure sand over the surface. Take from the plants a number of the young side shoots, or, from the chief branches cut the short shoots that look fresh and green and in a growing state. Trim off all the leaves, except a few at the top, and dibble the cuttings in very close together, and in such a small compass] that you can cover them over with a hand-light or one of Philips's propagators. Water them moderately with a fine rose, and at once put the glass over, and strew an inch depth of coal-ashes all round it outside—say for a breadth of four inches next the frame all round—this will enable you to give air when necessary without permitting the entrance of slugs.

At the end of a week look over the cuttings, and pull out any that appear to be failing, because, if they are allowed to rot amongst the others, they may spread infection. Leave the glass tilted for an hour to air them, and then shut close again. After that, give air regularly, keep moderately moist, and in about six weeks the cuttings will be rooted. Pot them off in small sixties, which are better than thumb-pots for Genistas, because they do not like to be frequently shifted. The soil should be peat and loam chiefly, with a little sand and leaf-mould added. Place them in a warm, shady place, and keep them only moderately moist for a fortnight—a cool pit would be the best place for them to gain strength—and as soon as they have made a start, it will be time to seek winter quarters for them.

A cool greenhouse is the proper place; but as they only require to be kept from frost, and will even winter out of

doors — the Canariensis especially, needing only a little
protection — a spare window in an attic may be assigned
them, and they must be kept as nearly dry as possible till
they begin to show signs of moving in spring.

By March they will be fairly on the move, and must have
a shift, and it should be at once to forty-eights, and in those
pots they may pass the summer, and in autumn the most
promising may go into thirty-twos, or even twenty-fours,
for blooming next spring. At this shift into the bloom-pots,
a little sweet old dung should be added to the compost, and
they should be wintered in as warm and light a place as you
an find for them, and they will bloom bravely as soon as
spring sets in. In giving them a gentle push towards
blooming, guard against exposing them either to extreme
cold or to the undue heat of a forcing-pit, or even the glow
of a bright winter fire. An equable mild temperature is the
thing for them, and damp must be remembered as a decided
enemy.

Genistas improve every year if kept in good shape, and
put out during the summer to ripen their shoots for blooming. They want no "coddling," no training up, and give
as little trouble as any choice flower that can be chosen as a
household god. The hardy ones all thrive in common loamy
soil, and are best planted out in early spring, when they
begin their seasonable growth. Most of them, hardy or
tender, come freely from seeds; and for this reason they
open a field for hybridizing that any lover of a garden may
profitably explore by way of experiment.

THE CHRYSANTHEMUM.

What a curiosity of nature is a Chrysanthemum? It sets
one thinking seriously to behold a crocus pertinaciously
blooming in the midst of frost and snow in spring, while a
chrysanthemum stands stock-still till the end of summer,

and then hurries into completed growth and blossom. Everything has its season, and our flower is given us to make the grand finale of the florist's year, which, in the words of Byron, must ever

"Rise, and shine, and set in glory."

Perhaps there is no more stubborn flower than a chrysanthemum: it will not be forced, but will have its own season of rejoicing; and, perhaps, if we could hurry it into bloom at any time we choose, as we do many other flowers, it would be far less welcome than in its own period of the sere and yellow leaf. Then it certainly is a glorious thing, reviving the brightness of the borders and giving light and life to the parterres, which a declining sun would otherwise render dingy and dolorous.

This is a flower which plays us no tricks—soot and smoke do not ruin it—drought does not destroy it; it is not particular as to soil or situation, and makes a gay show if ever so much neglected. Look at the town plot, how it rejoices in chrysanthemums—look at the London squares, and above all, at the Temple Gardens, and see how this universal favourite defies the evil influences that crush roses, pansies, carnations, and a hundred other things that are worth any price if we can have them.

Still, though the chrysanthemum has a strong constitution, it is not to be abused—there is a right and a wrong way of growing it, as of most other things. In the first place, the stock is to be obtained by cuttings from good sorts: they are to be carefully rooted and tenderly planted out. This portion of the work may be done at any time from April to the middle of August. Make your cuttings from strong stems, and nip off the tops so as to shorten them to three or four woody joints; dibble them into finely-sifted sandy loam, in which a little old dung is mingled. Shade them for a week or ten days, and keep all moist, and by that time the cuttings will be well rooted. The open ground does very well for the purpose, but a cold frame does better. In the absence of a frame, prepare a shady nook with suitable compost, or if you cannot find a shady place, make a shade with a few boards, or one or two hurdles covered with straw.

Supposing the reader to have some good plants pushing forward towards bloom, he may even now increase the stock by layering some of the top shoots. Select those that have a goodly number of side branches, layer them into forty-eight-size pots, or take them off and pot them as cuttings; give plenty of water and close shadow for a week; then admit the light by degrees, and as soon as they begin to make head, plant them out carefully where they are to bloom, and before Christmas they will, like the Crimean generals, be " covered with glory."

As to the sort of soil in which the plants are to be bloomed, let it be light and rich. This is a plant which blooms very freely in the worst of soils, and with the worst of treatment; but, it scarcely need be said that a *good* chrysanthemum is only to be obtained by the exercise of proper skill in its cultivation.

Now, in the growth of the plants after they are rooted depends the kind of blossom you will have. The chrysanthemum makes a huge bunch of fibrous roots very near the surface, and it is evident that unless this habit of the plant be conquered a little, it must suffer from the frequent play of the hot sun on the surface fibres. Hence, it is very common to mulch them with fresh dung, and with established plants this is a good practice—the rains wash down the soluble parts of the manure to nourish the plants, and the moist material preserves coolness at the root, and prevents the deterioration of the plant by drought.

But though mulching is in a general sense good, the plan I have for many years followed I think better. I take my stock of plants from the frame when well rooted and plant them out as follows:—I first take out a quantity of mould from the chosen spot and make a deep hole. Into that I throw first two or three spadesful of half-rotted dung, of the

same kind as I should choose for manuring cabbages—that
is to say, it is rather rank and very moist, and would injure
any choice flowers if it came into contact with them. Upon
this I put a layer of leaf-mould and sand well mingled, and
on this top layer I carefully fix the roots of the chrysanthemum. When all are planted, I water well to settle the
earth about the roots, and the next day rake over neatly.
For a time the plants root into the top stratum and form a
tough nest of fibres, but the dung below attracts the roots,
and by the time the plants begin to form flower-buds the
roots have reached it: they are protected from drought, and
they draw from the manure a nourishment which enables
them to bloom freely and finely, and without any loss of
character. New dung would certainly not do, nor would
half-rotted dung be suitable, unless it were turned over two
or three times to sweeten it, and exhaust its heat before
using it.

Even with this plan of deep manuring, mulching is also
useful, and the best material for the purpose is short dung
covered with a thin layer of fine leaf-mould to preserve a
cleanliness of appearance and lightness of texture.

In the general culture it will be noticed that crysanthe-
mums make a quick growth in early spring, and their fresh
verdant heads are then useful in the borders, in giving contrast to the gay plants that stand before them. After a
time they halt in their progress, and from May to July grow
very slowly—in fact, keep almost at a stand-still. While
they remain in this comparatively dormant condition they
are forming pulp out of which to manufacture blossoms; and
to aid them in this important process, mulching and watering
are resorted to. If the earth round them gets caked into a
hard mass, first loosen it with a fork and remove the top
stratum. Replace this with the best mulching material you
have at hand, and twice a week during dry weather water
them liberally with manure-water. · This may be pretty
strong, and made either from guano or by steeping new dung

in a tub of rain water, and drawing off the liquid as
required.

As the plants advance they must be well secured, by
means of stakes, for the July storms frequently make sad
havoc with these as well as with dahlias and hollyhocks,
when the staking has been neglected. As soon as the flower
heads begin to show, thin them out, and trim the plants into
elegance of shape; for the more blooms the smaller will they
be, but by the practice of high culture and severe thinning
of the blossoms, they may be brought to almost any size you
desire.

June and July are the best seasons for propagating the
chrysanthemum, by cuttings; but, as we have just re-
marked, it may be done now if not a day be lost. With
regard to old plants, it must be borne in mind that they
rapidly exhaust the soil, and are improved by being
separated and transplanted in March and April. If left
to grow into huge bushes they lose character, get exhausted
in a few years, and either perish or become worthless. They
require to be grown liberally, and are sure to repay the little
trouble they occasion in manuring and watering, and occasional transplanting.

The pot culture of the chrysanthemum differs little from
its treatment in the open ground. Here the gay pompons
come into legitimate use, and what can be finer for a
drawing-room or parlour window than a few potted pompons, in full bloom, studded with bright buttons of almost
every tint of the rainbow. Florists have lately done their
best to sneer the pompons out of culture, but public opinion
is against them, and the pretty pompons enjoy as much fame
as ever. The larger sorts may be pomponed, so to speak, by
striking them late, putting them into small pots, with rather
poor soil of a sandy nature, and shifting them *once* only for
blooming, and then into pots as small as they can be got
into. On this plan they bloom freely, and the blossoms
acquire a neatness of shape and brightness of colour,

especially if the plants are grown as *slowly* as possible, till the last moment, and are then stimulated into profusion of bloom by means of liquid manure.

THE CALCEOLARIA.

Among the flowers that must now have attention is the Calceolaria. Though a universal favourite, the Calceolaria is sadly abused in the treatment to which it is subjected at all seasons. Some set them out to perish on window-sills and on flower-stands; others force them in winter by the aid of a fierce heat, only to see them languish, and at last perish, just as they ought to bloom; while others who feel proudly their power to pay, make a yearly sacrifice of their stock rather than acquire the skill necessary to preserve it throughout the winter season.

The Calceolaria has a natural habitat very closely resembling that of the Alpine Auricula. It is a native of high latitudes, it loves abundance of light, will stand a very low temperature, and is accustomed, when at home, to have its feet frequently bathed with snow-water. It will not bear extremes of any kind, but luxuriates most in a medium temperature and a cool moist soil; hence its adaptability for bedding, and its comparative hardihood when kept cool and moist in summer, and merely sheltered from frost in winter.

This being the time for making cuttings, I should advise the possessor of good plants to wait till the middle or end of the month, and then, as the plants go out of bloom, to select the ripest shoots, and strike them in pots in a cold frame, or in a very shady border. Plenty of sand should be used, but not a particle of leaf-mould; the pots should be kept always liberally moist after the first ten days, and if a slip of window-glass, or a bell-glass, is placed over each pot, the cuttings will root the faster.

The most important matter in raising calceolarias, whether
of the shrubby or herbaceous kinds, is to keep them always
moist without being wet at the roots, and to plunge the pots
to prevent the sun from heating them. Dryness is ruin,
and excessive heat, at any season, dangerous at the very
least.

Towards October, the young plants will be ready for their
first removal. For this purpose use a rich, light, ·sandy
soil, very sweet, and free from recent dung or tree-leaves.
The young plants should be wintered in four-inch pots, and
the house should be but moderately heated. If there is no
means of wintering them in a cool greenhouse, it may be
borne in mind that calceolarias will winter out-of-doors, if
made secure against frost by means of a cold frame, or even
the slight shelter of a few boards set towards the north. So
long as they are kept at a temperature only two or three
degrees above freezing-point, they will do well, and make
very strong plants. If wintered with other stock, such as
fuchsias, geraniums, &c., the heat of the house will generally be too much for them, so that it will be best not only
to give them the coolest place that can be found, but also to
plunge the pots into larger ones, containing damp moss; or,
better still, to fill a large box with moss or ashes, and plunge
the pots into this to the rim, keeping the whole moist by
means of the fine rose of a watering-pot. If the plants are
forward, they will throw up trusses of bloom much too soon,
and this must be prevented by frequent re-potting, and every
head of bloom that shows before May should be pinched off,
and the plants potted, to give them a check. By regulating
the potting as to time, and the progressive sizes of the pots,
the plants may be grown to an immense size; and, as
April approaches, they should be potted for blooming through
the summer. It will be better, however, to keep back a few
of the least forward plants, and pot them for the last time
in the first week of June, to make a succession late in the
season.

Calceolarias are easily raised from seed, and this is a better way of maintaining and improving a stock than by cuttings. The great difficulty, however, is to obtain the seed ; for even if saved by the grower from the finest specimens, the produce may be of a worthless description. This saving of seed is really a delicate matter, and requires a nice discrimination to prevent disappointment. The seeds should be taken only from the strongest plants, of good shrubby habit, clear colour, and in which the blossoms are entirely without crumples. If it is intended to hybridize, sorts should be chosen that possess special qualities—one perhaps being selected for its handsome habit, and another for its splendour of bloom.

August is certainly the best season for getting in the seeds. Many sow in June and July, but such early sowing is objectionable—the plants get too forward before winter, and make many attempts to bloom in spring before it would be advisable to allow them. The sowing should be carefully performed, and proper precaution taken to prevent the access of slugs to the seedlings. A few hand-lights, placed on a bottom of coal-ashes, in a shady place, is the best seed-bed. Let the seed be sown in six-inch pots, in which there is plenty of drainage, the top soil being formed of sandy loam and sifted leaf-mould. Having watered the pots, press

down and cover the seeds, and place the lights over. The
whole should be kept moist, and no air admitted till the
seedlings are up, and then the lights must be lifted to prevent damping off. Give more air by degrees, and as soon
as the plants are large enough to handle, prick them out
into pots or shallow pans, and treat them in the same way
as already directed for cuttings. If properly wintered, they
will make large plants by May.

If a supply of plants in bloom be wanted in the ensuing
May, October is the proper time to prepare them, by shifting
them into larger pots ; but the main stock should be pricked
out till large enough for separate pots, and then regularly
shifted and rather kept back by a cool temperature than
hastened into premature growth. The folly of hurrying the
calceolaria is seen in the fact, that the weakest autumn
plants usually make the strongest heads of bloom in spring,
and endure better as bedders.

As to sorts, calceolarias naturally separate themselves into
two great groups, the shrubby and the herbaceous. The
first kind supplies us with the gay bedders, which make the
purest yellow for grouping of any choice plant we possess.
The herbaceous sorts are usually bloomed in pots, and are
distinguished from the former by the large size and variety
of tint of their blossoms, which rise on long flower-stalks.
The shrubby sorts are more profuse in bloom, the flower-
stems are shorter, and the whole aspect of the plant is
fresher, heartier, and more robust. But another great distinction between them is seen in the permanence of the
blooms in the shrubby sorts ; whereas the herbaceous kinds
bloom by fits and starts, and require careful treatment to
ensure a regular succession of trusses, each of which is the
result of a separate effort.

Mr. Fisk defines a good specimen to be one in which the
foliage makes a fine background for the flowers. "The
larger the flower the better it will be, provided it is circular
in outline, without crumples or serratures, and convex or
globular in shape instead of flat: the mouth of the purse

cannot be too small," and the colours, whether of a self or
a spotted sort, very clear and distinct.

As florists' flowers, the herbaceous and semi-herbaceous
are all of them noble plants. It would be difficult to find,
among the hundreds of old and the dozens of new sorts,
one that may not be regarded as a beautiful object, even
if the laws of floriculture forbid us to regard it as perfect.
But none of these suit for bedding. To make our grand
patches of gold colour, the old shrubby sorts only will do,
however fine many of the kinds are which have been produced by hybridising.

THE CINERARIA.

This window pet is a sort of companion to the Chinese
primula; both come into bloom together, but the primulas
are exhausted while the Cinerarias are yet in their prime.
The glory of the cineraria is its intensely vivid colours; a
stage of show plants being unequalled by anything else in
the florist's long list for dazzling crimsons, blues, browns,
and violets. Even a poor cineraria is a pretty thing, because
its flowers are always abundant; they come at a season when
every flower is precious, because scarce; and they go out
just in time to be succeeded by pelargoniums, fuchsias, and
all sorts of true summer things.

The Cineraria is one of the many high-class flowers which
prove to be so nearly hardy, that everybody may cultivate
them. There are geraniums, calceolarias, fuchsias, genistas,
pansies, auriculas, and numerous others that may be brought
to good condition, with either very little artificial heat, or
none at all; and these are the sort of flowers that I prefer
to treat of in these pages, in the hope that thousands of
readers will take to floriculture in earnest, when shown
what may be done with very simple means.

I shall suppose that you have a few cinerarias that have
just done blooming. Those that were really good, save;

those that were poor or only middling, throw away; for it is a waste of time to propagate anything of a second or third-rate character. As soon as your good plants begin to look shabby, cut off the flower-stems, and trim out any flower-

THE CINERARIA.

buds that may be pushing from below; it would be a folly to let them bloom any longer, because the plants would be exhausted. Prepare a bed of coal-ashes in an open shady place, and on this bed range the pots containing the plants. If any offsets have risen and grown pretty strong, slip them off very neatly with a sharp knife, taking care that you have as much root as belongs to them, and then pile up round the stem of each of the old plants a little cone of fine sandy mould, the more sandy the better. Pot the offsets at once into small pots, water them, and place them in a cold frame, on a bed of ashes; shade them for a fortnight, and by that time they will be well rooted.

In the meantime, the old plants will from the base of the stem put out fibres into the sandy soil that was plied round the collar of each, and numerous offsets will break through, each of which must be slipped off when possessed of two or more leaves, and potted as just described. In this way, every good plant will give you from half-a-dozen to a dozen young ones, and you will have stock to start with.

When the offsets have been potted about three weeks, they will require shifting into pots a size larger, and though at the first potting any light fibrous sandy soil will do—and there ought to be plenty of sharp silver-sand mixed with it—at the next potting they must have a soil specially prepared for them, and this soil must be compounded thus:—Get some turfy loam from an upland pasture, some two-year old leaf-mould, and some fibrous peat, some very rotten cow-dung, some river-sand, and plenty of broken potsherds in various sizes, some being as small as peas. In making up the compost, use turfy loam two bushels, peat, leaf-mould, and cow-dung one bushel each, and half a bushel of sharp river-sand. The compost must be well chopped up, and brought to a friable condition, in fact, made as fine as it can be *without sifting*. Never sift your soil unless specially directed to do so; the practice has marred many a good man's work, who thought that fine flowers and fine soil were necessarily related to each other. From the time the plants have this second potting, they grow steadily, and must never get pot-bound. To know when to shift them, turn one out carefully, and ascertain the state of the roots; if they fill the pot, then the plant must have a pot a size larger, and so

L

on till they get into eight-inch pots for blooming, but of that presently. Beware of one error common to beginners, never place a choice plant in a pot larger than it can fill in a few weeks; the secret of success is in the succession of shifts, one size larger each time, except in the case of such plants as do not bear shifting at all, very few of which are classed as " florist's flowers."

Another mode of raising young stock is by seed. This should be sown during May and June, if purchased; and if raised at home from choice specimen plants, sow it the moment it is sufficiently ripe. The best way to sow it is to procure some shallow pans, fill them with fine light soil, water moderately, sprinkle the seed thinly on the surface, and just cover with silver-sand. In a cold pit they will soon come up needing no artificial heat. As soon as the seedlings have two or three leaves, prick them out into small pots in a similar light soil, adding a little leaf-mould to nourish them; and as soon as they fill these small pots with roots, shift them to a size larger and use the compost just described. From this time seedlings and offsets need the same treatment. If the seed is really good, the seedling plants will make the finest show at blooming time—there is nothing like sowing seed if you want variety in florist's flowers. They come of all colours in endless profusion, and they have, generally, greater strength than plants propagated from offsets or cuttings.

By this time Jack Frost will be making an occasional morning call, and your cinerarias must be prepared to pass through the winter safely. Though these plants are generally wintered in greenhouses, it should be borne in mind that they cannot stand any amount of heat—in fact, they winter best in a common cold frame well banked up with litter or dry fern, to keep the frost from penetrating at the sides and ends. Give them a shift as they require it, using always plenty of drainage, and putting over the layer of broken pots, some of the rougher parts of the compost to prevent the soil from washing down and causing them to be water-logged. There are few things that root faster than the cineraria, so you must keep a sharp look-out to give them room as they require it. Every move is a slight check that causes the plant to grow dwarf and compact, at the same time the additional root-room given strengthens the formation of the trusses of bloom, which should ultimately rise up in dense heads from close-growing broad-leaved, healthy-looking plants. They are very brittle, and in potting must be handled tenderly, as every injury leads to a loss of sap which deteriorates the plant, and causes imperfect blowing.

When winter has fairly set in, every necessary precaution must be taken to prevent injury from frost. In severe weather the frames must be covered with mats night and day, and even litter or fern added to that, if the frost should be intense; for although they repudiate heat, they also flinch before frost, and once seriously attacked, never recover. Every fine day give air and light; but rather than let frost into the frames, they may be kept covered up for a fortnight together; though, of course, that is not advisable unless the case is desperate. By having the plants strong and healthy and well aired up to the last moment, and then kept as dry and clean as possible, there will be little fear of losses through frost, if the precautions that we advise be adopted in time.

As soon as the first blush of spring calls vegetation to its seasonal renewal, bring your cinerarias to the greenhouse and give them a cool place very close to the glass. If you have no greenhouse, let them remain in the frames, or bring the forwardest indoors to complete their growth in the windows. Now the flower stems will push rapidly from your healthy large-leaved plants. Those that want opening and supporting with sticks must be neatly banded; but if for exhibition, all such supports must be removed a day or two before the show, or your plants may be looked upon as cripples ; and, in fact, show flowers that need sticks usually *are* cripples. You have now only to wait, and the reward for your care will be worthy your acceptance. A good cineraria should have a solid truss, the flowers touching each other, and forming one grand globular mass of intensely bright colour. Each individual flower should be nearly or quite circular, and the less the florets divide around the edge the better ; in fact, a model flower should be as completely circular as a florin, with no visible indentations on the edge, the central disk measuring one-third of the entire diameter, and the colour, whatever it is, decided and brilliant. Even finely coloured flowers are apt to come loose and with deep divisions between the florets. We have yet to bring the cineraria to the very perfect and unbroken circle that the florist demands of it.

A few words must be said as to the diseases and pests of this flower. The cineraria is a *soft* wooded plant, and like all others of that kind, is apt to " damp off," that is, to rot where the plant meets the surface of the mould. Silver sand strewed on the surface is a good preventive of damping ; but the grand point is to give air and water judiciously—only as much of the latter as the plants really require—it is the excess, causing coldness and stagnation of the sap, that causes " damping," which is a rare calamity in the stock of an assiduous grower.

Green-fly is a very common pest of the cineraria : the great preventive in this case is to grow the plants as hardy as possible, " codled" plants being always most readily affected. Tobacco smoke soon settles the fly, but any excess of it is a great injury to this succulent plant, which really has a poor power of resisting on account of its moist absorbent nature—it has no woody fibre to fall back upon, and hence, though comparatively hardy, will not bear with impunity any extremes of treatment or any very violent attack of its enemies. Those who intend to follow these instructions in raising cinerarias for blooming next spring, have the best season before them. Set to work directly, get your plants into good shape before winter sets in, and you may herald in the next spring in a manner worthy of the coy but welcome maiden.

THE SNAPDRAGON.

Who, that has ever enjoyed a summer ramble among the ruins of an old castle or a decayed monastery, but must have experienced that strange feeling of mingled sadness and delight which is the invariable accompaniment of the spectacle of " art in ruins," in every mind capable of refined contemplations ?

The Snapdragon, or *Antirrhinum*, is one of the very best of our hardy herbaceous perennials; a great favourite and old friend in the cottage garden, but a very fit ornament to the borders of a princely lawn. It is capable of assuming innumerable varieties; hence the interest attaching to its culture, apart from its intrinsic beauty.

The mother plant of most of the cultivated Antirrhinums is *A. majus*, a species which has pink flowers, a native of Britain, and very commonly met with on old walls and ruins. About Rochester castle there is abundance of it. Of *A. majus* there are four distinct sorts—namely, *bicolor* (two-coloured); *coccineus* (scarlet); *flore pleno* (double-flowered); and *variegatum*, which has very prettily variegated leaves. Besides these there are hundreds of named varieties which rank as very favourite florist's flowers. It is in this *A. majus* section that the greatest number of cultivated varieties occur; and the amateur should, therefore, save seed of the best of his plants, with a view to obtain new sorts. Among the foreign species, we have *asarina*, a native of Italy, white; *glandulosum*, from California, roan; *medium* and *meananthum*, both from the south of Europe, pink; *molle*, a trailing species from Spain, white; *sempervirens*, the evergreen snapdragon from the Pyrenees, pink; and *Siculum*, from Sicily, white. All these are worth the attention of those who might be desirous of forming a collection; there are many other species that need not be enumerated here.

The month of July is just the time to commence the culture of the *Antirrhinum:* stock may then be purchased to advantage, because the plants are now in bloom, and may be chosen as they please the eye of the purchaser, and from the first of the month to the middle of August they may be propagated from either seeds or cuttings; indeed, from cuttings they may be increased up to the end of September. Suppose you get your first stock in bloom from a nursery, you will then either keep them in their pots for any out-door decorations you may wish them for, or adopt the better plan of bedding them out. Here it is that the snapdragon shows its beauty—it is a lovely border flower—it is one of the best of things for a rockery, a raised bank, a retired nook under trees, or on the top of a wall or along the coping of a shed, and, strange to say, it will do equally well in either position; but high-bred florist's kinds should, of course, not be harshly dealt with. The most shrubby and desirable plants may be propagated at once. Prepare a bed of light sandy soil, in which there should be incorporated some old mortar broken into fragments of the size of walnuts, and also a moderate proportion of broken crocks of the same size. The soil must be light and porous, for these plants will not well stand wet, otherwise a special compost is quite unnecessary—common garden soil is all they require. Take from the plants as many side shoots as can be spared, trim off the lower leaves and insert the cuttings in patches over the bed, so arranged that each patch can be covered with a hand-light. If you have no hand-lights, shade them for a week with empty pots inverted, or plunge a few pots in any spare place; let the pots be half-filled with sandy soil and a few crocks intermingled; dibble the cuttings inside the pots, so that they touch the pots all round, and cover each with a bit of window-glass. If kept moderately moist they will be rooted in three weeks, and may then be potted or planted to stand the winter.

In potting, use plenty of drainage at the bottom of the pot, and then fill up with any friable soil in which you have previously blended some very small crocks and fragments of old mortar or broken freestone. If the plants are of really high merit, use a little extra care, and give them an inch of well-rotted dung over the top of the soil, and on that a sprinkling of silver-sand. It is a rule in flower-growing that the higher the breeding of a plant the more tender it is; hence high-bred and named sorts should be wintered in a cold pit on a bed of ashes, and all through the winter they should have as much air as possible, but be sufficiently protected against frost. About the middle of the March following, those potted in the autumn should be planted out for flowering; or, if to be grown into specimens for exhibition, shift them on and nip off every truss of bloom that appears until quite the end of June, so as by that time to have them in large pots in which they are to be allowed to bloom.

When planted out, the hardy varieties need no special care; the flower-stems should be cut off as soon as the blooms. get shabby, unless seed is required, and then it should be saved from the first truss of bloom that appears, and no other trusses should be allowed to open. The seed will ripen early, and may be saved in the usual way till the March following.

Antirrhinums raised from seed generally bloom the first season, if sown on a gentle heat early in March, and then pricked out and hardened off by degrees, and turned out into the borders in May. If you have no heat, it will be better to defer sowing till June; and from the 1st of June to the 1st of August it may be sown with a certain prospect of success, and the plants will have full time to attain strength to go through the winter safely. Sow on a light sunny border in similar soil as that recommended for cuttings, and first cover the seed with a layer of silver-sand. Prick them out when large enough to handle, and choose showery weather for the operation; if sown thick, they should be thinned out early to prevent the plants from rising spindled: the removal will give them a check that will cause them to grow stubby and strong; for you should always aim at large blooms on dwarf bushy plants in every one of your efforts at choice flower culture. Seed saved from fine specimen blooms should be raised with a little extra care.

Prepare a little good potting mould, say one-third equal parts leaf-mould and very rotten dung, one-third common soil of the garden, and one-third very small crooks, old mortar, and silver sand. In this very fine plants may be produced. If they are potted into the smallest pots as soon as they have four good leaves, and from that time potted on in regular shifts, till within a month of their time of blooming, then they may be allowed to get pot-bound, and have a little very weak manure-water once a week till the blossoms open. After that give pure water only, and when they go out of bloom trim them up, take off what cuttings you require, and put them into small pots again, cutting in the roots a little, and proceed as before. Those planted out should be taken up every three years and the soil renewed, plenty of drainage being used on every occasion of potting or planting, for this flower suffers from damp as soon as any.

THE PETUNIA.

The Petunia came from Buenos Ayres in 1831, and created a little sensation here, when *P. phœnicea*, the first one introduced, displayed its lovely purple flowers. Shortly afterwards another species, *P. violacea*, was introduced, which had small violet-coloured flowers, and attracted great attention; and at last the two hybridized, and produced the various shades of blue, lilac, purple, and rose, and then the petunia became a florist's flower.

To grow the petunia to perfection is a work requiring skill, judgment and patience; though for ordinary greenhouse, window, and garden exhibition, a stock may be got up as easily as verbenas, but certainly not so easily as geraniums and calceolarias, which are the simplest of all things to multiply by the thousand.

The best soil for the petunia, when grown as a pot-plant, is a compost of a light, rich, open character, and to make a heap for the purpose proceed as follows :—Get some turf

from an upland pasture, lay it up and turn it over for a year at least, then add to it an equal quantity of sweet leaf-mould and peat earth from a dry moor, with a liberal addition of river or silver sand. This is the perfection of a compost, and will do for many other soft-wooded plants besides petunias. If it is not within your means to make such a compost, and to wait a year for its preparation, take crumbly peat, yellow loam, leaf-mould, and very rotton cow-dung and silver sand in equal quantities, mix them well, and in potting add a few pieces of charcoal to keep the soil open.

The propagation of the petunia is conducted in much the same way as the pansy; it comes from seeds and cuttings, but must be ordinarily treated as an annual. The seeds may be sown in shallow pans in a moderate heat in February, pricked off as they come on into four-inch pots, then potted in sixties, and shifted regularly till they bloom. During their growth they may be frequently stopped, and the points put in as cuttings; but as soon as the plants have flowered out, they may be flung away, unless seed is wanted, for it is a folly to attempt to keep stock of old plants through the winter; they will worry you to death to keep them alive till January, and then, in spite of you, will perish.

For greenhouse culture, there is nothing like raising new stock in autumn. The young shoots strike easily in sand in a cold pit, and require no protection from bell-glasses, merely shading from the hot sun. Some folks keep them in the cutting-pots all winter, but fine plants are never produced in that way; they ought to be potted off as soon as rooted, shaded, and moderately watered till well established; and then consigned to a shelf near the glass in the greenhouse; and with two or three pottings in spring, and stopping every shoot at the third joint, magnificent plants may be produced to bloom the summer through. But if the cultivator has a fear as to their safe wintering, he may begin in February. The cuttings must be put in in the usual way, and the pots plunged in bottom heat and kept close for a short time; they soon root, and must then be potted off. Place them in heat again to give them a start, and as soon as they begin to grow, top them, and put in the tops as cuttings. In the same way stop every shoot, and keep on shifting as the plants increase in size, but always guard against excess of moisture. Too dry rather than too wet is the rule for growing petunias. As they get established, light and air must be given freely, and but little heat will be needed as spring advances. As they become bushy, peg them out; if this is neglected, they grow towards the centre, and will soon be ruined. Shift again, and continue stopping at the third joint, and as they begin to show bloom, water occasionally with weak liquid manure. On no account let them suffer for want of pegging down and tying out; there is nothing more slovenly than to let plants "grow any how," till they are past trimming, and then to put them in order by forcing their shoots this way and that. They must be kept open and orderly at every stage, and the light will have free play on every stem, and every part of a stem, and your reward will be seen when blooming time comes.

By this plan you may make successional shifts, starting with three-inch pots and ending with eight-inch, and by the middle of May or beginning of June, your plants ought to measure three feet in diameter, and eighteen inches high, with fine foliage down to the pot, and abundance of bloom from head to foot, superb specimens of floricultural art. As they open they should be placed in saucers, kept constantly full of liquid manure, for *then* you have nothing to fear in giving them abundance of moisture. A light sprinkling over the foliage in the morning will do them good, and if you mean to exhibit, you ought to pinch off every bloom till within ten days of the exhibition, giving plenty of air and sun meanwhile, and for the remainder of the period shading them during mid-day.

CPSIA information can be obtained at www.ICGtesting.com
Printed in the USA
BVOW06s0125050915

416575BV00024B/876/P